CONTENTS

Foreword

By Dayton Moore

Congratulations and thank you, Royals fans! Congratulations and thank you, Royals fans! This team—our team—took all of us on an incredible ride in 2014. We fell short of our goal of winning the World Series, but it was special to see this team come together and to see this city rally around our players.

Although I began working for the Royals in the summer of 2006, this journey for me really began, as it did for many of you, with the championship teams of the 1970s and '80s. The Kansas City Royals were the first team that I fell in love with growing up. I was born in Wichita, and although our family moved around the country, I always followed the Royals, thanks largely to the affection my grandmother held for the team and passed along to me.

The championship years culminated with the 1985 season, which I'll never forget. Dave Larson, a teammate of mine at Garden City Community College, and I watched Game 7 of the World Series from a grassy area between I-70 and the stadium. We were returning to Garden City from Illinois, where we had spent fall break. We thought we'd stop at the stadium and buy tickets for that night's game. Can you imagine? We thought we could walk up and buy tickets to the final game of the World Series! We quickly found out that we couldn't afford them, but there were plenty of people watching from the interstate, so we decided to join them. From

that spot we could see everything except Lonnie Smith in left field. But to this day, the thing that stood out most was the energy of the crowd. The stadium was electric.

That feeling was duplicated during this 2014 postseason run, from the wild-card game against Oakland through Game 7 of the World Series against San Francisco. Our fans at Kauffman Stadium were amazing. We certainly had a home-field advantage. As important, though, was the excitement all of our fans showed throughout greater Kansas City, the Midwest, and the nation. As an organization we felt that. Our players felt that. On the flip side, the joy, excitement, and energy that this team's run brought to each of you is special. Really, that's the essence of professional sports for a community.

The 2014 Royals were an exciting team to watch. I think Ned Yost did an outstanding job of creating a close camaraderie between these 25 guys and putting them in a position to win. Was every move he made successful? No, but that's the way it is for every manager. That's the way it is for general managers.

When we arrived in 2006, we knew we had to build our farm system while putting a competitive team on the field. We have missed with a few players, but our scouting and player personnel departments have done an incredible job of selecting players who best fit what we are trying to do here. In order to be

OUT OF THE

Blue

THE **KANSAS CITY ROYALS'** HISTORIC 2014 SEASON

This book is book is available in quantity at special discounts for your
group or organization. For further information, contact:

Triumph Books LLC
814 North Franklin Street
Chicago, Illinois 60610
Phone: (312) 337-0747
www.triumphbooks.com

Printed in U.S.A.
ISBN: 978-1-62937-118-4

Content packaged by Mojo Media, Inc.
Joe Funk: Editor
Jason Hinman: Creative Director

Front and back cover photos by USA TODAY Sports Images

successful for the long haul, one thing we've stressed since Day One is developing homegrown talent and then doing everything we can as a front office to support their efforts in winning.

That was a culmination of what you saw in 2014. Coming out of spring training, knowing that we had made big strides in 2013, we liked this team. We knew we'd likely have to make adjustments with the roster, but we felt key pieces were in place. We didn't expect it to be all rosy, and it wasn't. But that's why this is a team sport—players have to pick each other up. This group of men did that. It was special for me to sit back and watch

these guys work toward the common goal of trying to win the World Series.

We fell short of that goal in 2014, but I hope and pray that this is just the beginning of being in a position to compete for a World Series every year.

For now, I hope you'll relive this wonderful season in Royals baseball through the images and stories Matt Fulks compiled on the following pages. I know I will.

— Dayton Moore
Royals senior vice president,
baseball operations/general manager

More than 10,000 Royals fans attended the season celebration hosted by the team at Kauffman Stadium on October 30. A few brought with creative signs to show their support for the 2014 American League champions. (AP Images)

Introduction

By Denny Matthews

"When it's your turn, when it's your year, you're going to win, and there's nothing you can do about it."

I'm not sure how many times I said that on the air during the second half of this 2014 season, but it's true. When it's your year—whether that means winning the league championship or winning the World Series, it's meant to be, almost as if it's preordained. Much like the Royals of 1980 and 1985, the 2014 Royals proved that to be true.

The clues pointing toward this being the year the Royals would make a postseason run started to become evident during their eight-game winning streak in early August that included, coincidentally, a three-game sweep of the San Francisco Giants at Kauffman Stadium. That streak, which was the second longest of the season, came two weeks after we got swept in Boston and then lost the first game of a series at Chicago. The Royals, at that time, were eight games back in the division. At the end of that eight-game winning streak, we were one-and-a-half games back. That's when you could begin to see the clues. You could see it in winning games in wacky ways or the opponent handing you a game that you had no right to win. That was happening night after night. What would seem to be an occasional accident was becoming more of a pattern.

You'll read later in this book a great example of that. It was a mid-September game at Kauffman Stadium against the White Sox. After losing three out of four to Boston at home and five of their previous seven, the Royals were two games back in the division and needed a win. The boys were trailing 3–0 in the seventh and then 3–2 in the ninth. In the bottom of the ninth, Terrance Gore and Jarrod Dyson both scored from second base without the ball leaving the infield. That's not something you see every day. But that's just one of the many clues proving that this was the Royals' year.

The Royals goal when the season started was to make the playoffs. When they made the playoffs, it eliminated a lot of the pressure. When they won the wild-card game against Oakland, that eliminated whatever pressure was left. And now they were loose and relaxed and running free in the underdog role. What followed, first with the Angels and then with the Orioles, was ridiculously easy. All the pressure was transferred to the opposing teams, and they were wound tight. Normally you have to fight your way through the postseason, but the Royals, unfettered by pressure, breezed through the American League playoffs.

Then came the Giants, the National League wild-card team. Both teams had been underdogs through their league playoffs, and now you had two very similar teams facing one another—a compelling matchup that, unfortunately, went the Giants' way thanks largely to an incredibly talented pitcher, Madison Bumgarner.

You're going to have stressful games, but a couple things happened for the Royals in the 2014 postseason. With the exception of Bumgarner for the Giants and

possibly Jon Lester with Oakland, the starters the Royals faced were very average. Out of 15 postseason games, Bumgarner and Lester were the only starting pitchers who really gave the Royals fits. The other thing, though, that made it relatively stress-free was our bullpen. Kelvin Herrera, Wade Davis, and Greg Holland were incredible all season. Manager Ned Yost said it perfectly when he made the statement that he could manage for 50 more years and not have an easier time managing than he did with those three guys at the back of the bullpen.

Going into the season, there was no way to see they were going to be that good. During spring training you lose Luke Hochevar, who was seen as the set-up guy, and Davis is thrown into that spot. As a result, Davis gave us as perfect a season as is humanly possible on the major league level. A major injury—and Hochevar was the only one on the team to suffer one—turned into probably the best relief season any pitcher has ever had in the majors. Holland also was close to perfect. So Ned could sit back and relax late in games. I'm not sure any manager has been able to experience such a stress-free last three innings. It was so much fun to watch every night.

Offensively, everything fell into place with hardly any adversity from spring training through Game 7 of the World Series. The closest the Royals came to adversity was that sweep in Boston and loss in Chicago that put them eight games back with about six weeks left in the regular season. They could've folded their tents and been done for the year.

Of course, through the postseason, we saw guys like Mike Moustakas, Eric Hosmer, and Lorenzo Cain, among others, really step up offensively and defensively.

There's no denying this incredible season for the Royals. Out of all the great teams we had here through the 1970s and '80s, this one went through the American League playoffs on a streak that can't be beaten, winning eight straight. And maybe it was appropriate that, after winning a do-or-die wild-card game, the Royals and the Giants faced each other in a winner-take-all Game 7. That's where the run ended for the Royals, but what a magical season the club gave us.

— Denny Matthews
  the voice of the Royals since the team's inception

After the 2014 Kansas City Royals came within one win of the team's second World Series championship, fans attending the October 30 rally at Kauffman Stadium showed their optimisim for the team's chances in 2015. (AP Images)

October 21, 2014 • Giants 7, Royals 1

A Giant Ace

Bumgarner Outduels Shields, Pence Launches First-Inning Homer

His nickname is "Big Game James," which would imply that he does well in big games. After his performance throughout the 2014 postseason, Royals fans are left wondering if James Shields' nickname just implies that he pitches in his teams' biggest games.

Heading into the World Series, Shields was 1–0 in three postseason starts for the Royals in 2014 with a 5.64 ERA. In those three starts, his longest outing was six innings against the Angels. The other two games were five innings apiece against Oakland and Baltimore. Before Game 1 of the World Series, Shields downplayed the numbers and revealed that he passed a kidney stone during the ALCS. Royals manager Ned Yost gave Shields a vote of confidence, pointing out how much Shields wanted to put his AL playoff games behind him.

Someone forgot to alert the San Francisco Giants, who spoiled the feel-good story of the Royals and snapped Kansas City's 11-game postseason winning streak (dating back to 1985) on the opening night of the World Series at Kauffman Stadium.

Shields struggled through the first inning Tuesday night with both the San Francisco batters and his own control. It looked as if this might not be Kansas City's night when the very first batter, Gregor Blanco, dropped a hit in front of center fielder Lorenzo Cain. With the way the baseball gods were working throughout the American League playoffs, that ball would've carried a few feet more or stayed in the air a few moments longer so Cain could make a diving catch. Instead, the ball dropped in, and three batters later, Pablo Sandoval roped a double that scored Blanco. The big blow of the inning was a 421-foot, two-run homer on a 3–2 pitch by Hunter Pence to center. Shields had the count even at 2–2, which brought the Kauffman Stadium crowd to its feet, but three pitches later, Pence gave the Giants a 3–0 lead. San Francisco got half of its total 10 hits in the 33-pitch first inning. Although he didn't walk any in the first, trying to perfectly place pitches against the free-swinging Giants, Shields threw a first-pitch strike to only two of the seven batters he faced in the top of the first.

"He's down 3–0, and then from that point—it was okay in the second and third but was laboring at times with the secondary stuff," Yost said. "Normally when he's really, really good, he's spotting his fastball well, and his change-up is dynamite, and he was really struggling to command his change-up tonight."

As has been the case throughout his three previous starts, Shields didn't look comfortable. Even in the second and third innings, when Shields retired San Francisco in order, the Giants struck the ball hard. Shields was taken out in the fourth inning after not retiring the first three batters he faced. He allowed five runs and seven hits.

Danny Duffy, making his first appearance since October 2 during the ALDS against Anaheim, relieved Shields and gave up one hit and two runs during his three innings.

By the time the Royals came up to hit in the bottom of the fourth, after Duffy's first inning, the Giants had given their postseason ace, Madison Bumgarner, a five-run cushion. That was more than enough. Bumgarner allowed only three hits and one run in seven innings. The lone run came on a homer in the seventh by Salvador Perez. That was the first run Bumgarner had given up in 21 consecutive World Series innings. That streak to start a World Series career is second only to Hall of Fame pitcher Christy Mathewson, who went 28 scoreless innings. Perhaps as impressive, Perez's home run ended Bumgarner's postseason road scoreless streak at 32⅔ innings.

Kansas City squandered a prime opportunity to end Bumgarner's streaks and perhaps change the complex-ion of the game much earlier. With the score 3–0, Omar Infante led off the third for Kansas City by reaching on an error by shortstop Brandon Crawford. Mike Mousta-kas then doubled to the right-field corner. Pence played the carom perfectly, which forced Infante to hold at third. The top two batters in the Royals lineup, Alcides Escobar and Nori Aoki, both struck out swinging. After Lorenzo Cain drew a walk, Eric Hosmer grounded out to second, ending the inning. Although Kansas City got only four hits in the game, the top four batters in the lineup went a combined 1-for-14. After the Royals failed to score in the bottom of the third, the Giants added two runs in the top of the fourth.

"Bumgarner, he was dynamite," Yost said. "We had an opportunity in the third, and I was really impressed with the way he fed off our aggressiveness and just worked up the ladder to get out of that jam. He was nails tonight."

Bumgarner is now 3–1 with a 1.40 ERA in 38⅔ in-nings this postseason. He's gone at least seven innings in all five outings, and the only time he's allowed more than five hits was on October 6 when the Washington Nationals got six hits and beat him in the ALDS.

Shields is now 1–1 with a 7.11 ERA in the 2014 postseason. In 19 innings he's given up 28 hits and 15 runs. Opponents against Shields are batting .337, which is highest among all Kansas City pitchers in the post-season. Still, after Game 1, Yost was quick to say that Shields is the Game 5 starter in San Francisco.

"He's very competitive, and he's a guy that when his stuff is right, he's dominant," Yost said. "He's like what you saw off Bumgarner tonight, that's James Shields. I've been in this game a long time and I've seen guys struggle two and three and four times and all of a sud-den come out and throw a fantastic game.

"But you have to know James Shields. You have to know that he's a tremendous competitor. He has the ability to make adjustments. Right now he just hasn't been as sharp as he has been. But with the extra rest and then coming back five days from now, we think will benefit him." ■

After hitting a two-run home run in the first inning, Giants' Hunter Pence runs the third base line past pitcher James Shields. Shields gave up five runs in the first four innings. (AP Images)

All Tied Up

Tensions Rise As Butler, Infante Help Even Series at 1-1

The chant started raining down from the Kauffman Stadium crowd of 40,446: "Billy Butler!" *Clap, clap, clap, clap, clap* "Billy Butler!" *Clap, clap, clap, clap, clap* "Billy Butler!"

Finally, at the, um, encouragement of others in the dugout, Butler went up a couple steps and tipped his cap.

"They were egging me on [in the dugout], but I definitely heard the crowd was yelling my name," said Butler, who had two key hits in the Royals' 7–2 win against the Giants in Game 2 of the World Series. "They told me to get out there and do it. It was one of those things where your teammates tell you to do it—you're going to get out there. And the fans received me well. It was an exciting time."

Usually a curtain call is reserved for a big home run late in the game or an outstanding pitching performance. Butler's tip of the cap came in the sixth inning—after a base hit. Well, maybe a little more important than just a base hit. With the game tied at 2–2, San Francisco starting pitcher Jake Peavy gave up a hit to Lorenzo Cain and then walked Eric Hosmer. As Butler, who has hit Peavy well throughout his career, waited on deck, Giants manager Bruce Bochy went to his bullpen and brought in Jean Machi. Butler greeted him with the RBI single that scored Cain and gave the Royals a 3–2

lead. Royals manager Ned Yost sent in Terrance Gore to run for Butler. And the chanting began.

If Butler hadn't been pulled from the game, he probably would've scored anyway. Two batters later Salvador Perez belted a double that scored Hosmer and Gore. Omar Infante, who was one of four regular starters without a home run this postseason, increased Kansas City's lead with a two-run homer into the Royals bullpen off Hunter Strickland. (Butler, Cain, and Nori Aoki have yet to hit a home run during the postseason.) The home run set off fireworks atop the crown scoreboard followed by some mini-fireworks at home plate as a frustrated Strickland started jawing with Perez. Players from both teams came out of their dugouts.

"I don't know what happened with that guy," Perez said. "We don't want to fight on the field. I'm not that kind of person, that kind of player. I just like to play hard, enjoy the game, and try to get a W for my team."

Perez and his mates were on their way to doing that. By the time they were finished in the sixth, the Giants used five pitchers in the inning, and the Royals scored five runs and took a 7–2 lead. That was the first time a team has used five pitchers in an inning of a World Series game since Whitey Herzog and St. Louis did it in Game 7 of the 1985 series against the Royals. The five

After the Royals scored five runs in the sixth, frustrated Giants pitcher Hunter Strickland shouts at Salvador Perez, who is held back by the home plate umpire. Perez maintains that he had no intention of fighting with Strickland. (AP Images)

runs scored by the Royals in the inning were the most they've scored in a single inning—and more than they'd scored in five games—this postseason.

"We felt like with our big sixth inning there we took a little momentum out of how they were playing," said Butler, whose contract is up at the end of this season. "They were playing really well and they continue to play well. But we showed them that we have fight in us, and I think they knew that already. But we stepped up big there as a team, and that gave us some confidence in that clubhouse."

For a brief moment early in the game, the team's confidence and certainly that of the Kauffman Stadium crowd, was shaken when Gregor Blanco led off the game with a home run to the right-field bullpen off Kansas City starter Yordano Ventura, who had thrown eight pitches to Blanco, all fastballs.

"A lot of times with all pitchers for me, the first inning is kind of a time when you go out, get your rhythm, get your timing, get yourself settled into the ballgame," Yost said. "Blanco fouled off a couple of really good pitches and then centered one up. That was one of those things where, as a manager, that doesn't really bother you. Just hold the fort from that point on, get your rhythm going, get yourself established, and then from the second inning roll. And that's exactly what he did."

Ventura gave up only one more run in the game, when the Giants scored in the fourth. Pablo Sandoval led off the inning with a double to the wall in dead center on a ball that glanced off the side of Cain's glove. After Hunter Pence grounded out, Brandon Belt doubled to right, scoring Sandoval and making it a 2–2 game. Just when it looked as if the Giants might be in the midst of a

big inning, it ended abruptly when Michael Morse flew out to Aoki in right. Belt strayed too far off second base on Aoki's high throw that Ventura picked up and threw out Belt at second.

The Royals got on the board in the bottom of the first inning with two outs when Cain doubled to left-center. Hosmer walked on four pitches, giving the Royals two runners on base for only the second time in the first two games of the series. Butler knocked his first hit of the game, this one to left that scored Cain from second and tied the game at 1–1. It was the Royals' first hit with runners in scoring position since Game 2 of the ALCS.

With the two hits, Butler's boosted his average to .273 in the postseason with seven RBIs.

"He is such a force in our lineup and he has been for years," said Yost. "He's a guy that is tremendously intelligent when it comes to hitting. He knows the opposing pitchers as well as anybody and he's got a great eye at the plate. Anytime Billy gets up in those situations, I feel great. I feel like he's going to get the job done, and again he did it. He came up big for us twice tonight." ■

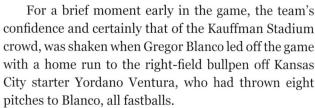

Above: First baseman Eric Hosmer dives onto the base to beat Gregor Blanco. Opposite: Omar Infante tags out Brandon Belt after catching him off base during the fourth inning. Infante also played an important offensive role in Game 2 with his two-run homer. (AP Images)

October 24, 2014 • Royals 3, Giants 2

A Pitchers' Duel

Veteran Guthrie, Royals Bullpen Thwart S.F. Giants

Jeremy Guthrie had pitched in 275 regular-season games and one postseason contest during his 11-year major league career. Tim Hudson had pitched in 458 regular-season games and 12 postseason games during a 16-year career. Neither had made a World Series appearance. That changed for both in the best pitching duel the Royals have had during this postseason.

But it'll be the 35-year-old Guthrie who'll never forget the night of October 24, 2014—the night he pitched one of the best games of his career and helped the Royals take a two games to one lead over San Francisco as the Royals beat the Giants 3–2 at AT&T Park.

"Happiness, excitement, gratitude—I think those describe it as best I can," Guthrie said. "It's something to have this chance. This opportunity is a tremendous blessing. To see a number of guys play a long time and don't get a chance to do this. So I'm very, very grateful for what the other 24 guys have done to put us in this position and what the other eight guys did tonight, plus the bullpen to help us win this one."

Guthrie gave up two runs and four hits over five innings. He didn't allow any walks or strike out any. Hudson, 39, went 5⅔ innings, giving up three runs and four hits. He struck out two and walked one. Guthrie

retired 10 in a row from the last out in the second until Brandon Crawford opened the sixth with a base hit. Hudson retired 11 in a row from the last out in the second until Alcides Escobar singled with one out in the sixth. During one stretch the two pitchers combined for 20 consecutive outs.

"[Hudson] had great stuff and was keeping the ball down, good movement on his pitches. I thought he did a really nice job. He gave us what we were hoping and a chance to win, and that's all you can ask for from your starters," said Giants manager Bruce Bochy. "But you look at their pitching, and they did a great job; they shut us down. We couldn't do too much off of Guthrie. He pitched great, and their bullpen did a good job. But as far as Huddy, I thought he got better and better as the game went."

The Royals employed the approach that's worked throughout this postseason: strong starting pitching, a shutdown bullpen, great defense, and timely hits.

The hits started early as Hudson left the first pitch of the game—a fastball, up—to Escobar, who jumped on it and launched it off the base of the left-field wall for a double. Alex Gordon, whom manager Ned Yost moved to the No. 2 spot in the lineup as he shifted things for the National League park, grounded the ball to first

Starter Jeremy Guthrie, who had a 4.31 ERA during the regular season, throws during the first inning. During Game 3, he allowed four hits and two runs. (AP Images)

and allowed Escobar to advance to third. Escobar then scored on a groundout to short by Lorenzo Cain, giving Kansas City an early 1–0 lead.

The Royals extended their lead in the top of the sixth. Escobar got his second hit of the night—the only Royals player with more than one—and broke Hudson's streak of 11 in a row. Gordon then lifted a double to center field over the head of Gregor Blanco and scored Escobar. That was Gordon's first World Series hit.

"It took a while, but it felt good," Gordon said. "With Esky getting on base, just trying to get a good pitch to hit, knowing if I hit it in the gap—with Esky's speed—he's more than likely to score. So it was a good at bat by Esky, and he got things rolling."

Two batters later after Cain grounded out and the Giants went with reliever Javier Lopez, Eric Hosmer battled through 11 pitches before lining one to center that scored Gordon and gave the Royals a 3–0 lead.

"That was a huge hit to finally break through and get the third run," Yost said. "It was a game-winning run right there. But I think it's more a testament to his tenacity in that situation, where he was not going to give in, and he was going to give his club the best at-bat that he possibly could. He kept fighting off pitches, kept fighting off pitches. He didn't get long. He didn't get strong. He was just trying to stay short up the middle, and finally got a pitch that he could do exactly that with."

The Giants made things interesting in the bottom of the sixth when Michael Morse grounded a double past a diving Mike Moustakas and into the left-field corner, scoring Brandon Crawford, who led off the inning with a hit. Yost decided to bring in Kelvin Herrera an inning earlier than usual. Herrera immediately walked Blanco

on four pitches. Joe Panik moved the runners to second and third with a high chopper to Herrera for the first out. Buster Posey cut the Royals' advantage to one run with a groundout to Omar Infante that scored Morse. With Blanco at third, Herrera escaped by inducing a groundout by Pablo Sandoval.

Herrera walked Hunter Pence to lead off the seventh inning and then struck out Brandon Belt before Yost went to the bullpen and brought in young Brandon Finnegan, who, remarkably, was pitching in the MLB World Series after pitching in the College World Series for TCU earlier this year. The Royals got back on track when Yost, with a 3–2 lead, brought in Wade Davis for the eighth and Greg Holland for the ninth.

"I'll just say when you have great defense and you have lock down bullpen pitching, you have a tendency to be in those types of games, and that's what we've had throughout the season," Guthrie said. "And fortunately for us right now, we've got guys throwing the ball great in the back end of the bullpen and able to hold on to these small leads."

Of course, to get to that lead, besides an offense to get some runs, it doesn't hurt to have a performance like Guthrie's, especially for his first World Series game. Even for an 11-year veteran, who admitted after the game that he stood behind the mound before his first pitch and looked around the stadium to soak in the moment.

"I've tried to do that throughout these playoffs," Guthrie said. "It felt like I was doing something that I didn't even dream of. A lot of people say they dreamed of playing in the World Series. I don't think I had that dream. But now to live it, it feels right and it feels like a moment that I'll never forget." ∎

Alcides Escobar is congratulated after scoring during the first inning, the first of three runs the Royals claimed for a Game 3 win. Escobar had a batting average of .285 in the regular season. (AP Images)

World Series: Game 4

October 25, 2014 • Giants 11, Royals 4

Royals Relievers Finally Falter

Duffy, Finnegan, and Collins Succumb to Giants' Hot Bats

Royals manager Ned Yost has answered questions until his face turned blue throughout this postseason about the comfort level of getting a game to the seventh inning with a lead or a tie and then turning the ball over to the unbeatable bullpen.

He and the Royals came up an inning short in Game 4 as the bullpen not named Herrera, Davis, and Holland was beatable—and, boy was it ever—in an 11–4 San Francisco win Saturday night at AT&T Park. The series is now tied at 2–2, which guarantees a return to Kansas City.

The Royals seemed to be holding their collective breath as they held a 4–2 lead with the Giants coming up in the fifth. Starter Jason Vargas, who looked shaky ever since his 27-pitch first inning, faced rookie Joe Panik, who led off the fifth with a double to right. With Danny Duffy and Jason Frasor ready in the bullpen and the heart of San Francisco's lineup scheduled to see Vargas for a third time, some questioned Yost's decision to start the inning with Vargas. Instead, after Panik's double, Yost then went to the pen and the right-handed Frasor against Buster Posey, who grounded out to Alcides Escobar but moved Panik to third. Hunter Pence, the wild-swinging right fielder who happens to be San Francisco's hottest hitter, singled past Escobar and scored Panik. The Royals held a 4–3 lead with one out and Pence at first. Yost decided to go with the left-handed Duffy to face Pablo Sandoval, forcing the switch-hitter to swing from his weaker right side.

It didn't work. Sandoval, who's been "Mr. October" for the Giants during their two recent World Series, sent a single to left. Pence, wisely electing not to test Alex Gordon's arm, remained at third. Juan Perez then tied the game at 4–4 with a sacrifice fly to center.

Vargas gave up three runs in his four innings of work.

"I didn't feel like [Vargas] was super sharp tonight, but he does what he does; he competes. I was really trying to get him through that fifth inning because I knew I'd have a hole there somewhere if we couldn't get him through," Yost said. "But with the two-run lead at that point, we decided to bring in Frasor, ended up giving up a base hit to Pence to make it 4–3, wanted to turn Panda around and hold that score right there, and try to find some way to get through the sixth inning to get to Kelvin [Herrera]. It just didn't work tonight. It doesn't work every night, you know. Most nights we do a pretty good job doing it. It just didn't work tonight."

That's an understatement. From the moment the game was tied at 4–4, it seemed as if the wheels were ready to come off for the Royals. And they did. Rookie Brandon Finnegan came in for Kansas City in the sixth inning and proceeded to give up back-to-back hits to pinch-hitter Joaquin Arias and Gregor Blanco. After Panik put down a sacrifice bunt that advanced Arias and Blanco 90 feet, Finnegan loaded the bases by intentionally walking Posey. The plan nearly paid off. Pence grounded the ball to Escobar, who fired it home to force Arias for the second out. But with two outs and the bases still full, Sandoval lined a two-RBI single to center, followed by an RBI single for Brandon Belt, giving the Giants a 7–4 lead.

Although that's all they needed, the Giants added four more runs in the bottom of the seventh.

Trailing 1–0 after the first, the Royals put together a very Royals-esque two-out rally in the third inning against San Francisco starter Ryan Vogelsong and seemed to have some control of the game. Gordon reached on a fielder's choice when the Giants recorded the second out of the inning, forcing Escobar at second base. With Lorenzo Cain at the plate, Gordon stole second. Cain then beat out an infield single to short that moved Gordon to third. Hosmer rolled a slow grounder between first and second that both Belt and Vogelsong originally tried to field. Vogelsong peeled off and tried to cover first but he missed the bag. Gordon scored on the play, tying the game at 1–1. After Vogelsong loaded the bases with a walk to Mike Moustakas, Omar Infante drove a 2–2 pitch up the middle that scored Cain and Hosmer, and gave the Royals a 3–1 lead. Salvador Perez added to the hit parade with an RBI single to center that scored Moustakas and chased Vogelsong. Through the first two innings, Vogelsong had thrown 28 pitches. He threw 34 in the third. That ended the scoring for the Royals as Vargas, who led off the inning with a fly out, made the third out when reliever Jean Machi struck him out on a 3–2 count. The Royals sent 10 to the plate and left the bases loaded during the 30-minute inning.

"Not really, no," Yost said, when asked if he felt good at that point. "We still had a lot of game to play. I've got a lot of respect for the Giants. I don't ever feel good even with the lead until we make the last out. So I knew that we had to continue to try to find ways to get outs and try to get to the seventh inning, tied or with the lead, to get to our main guys."

The Royals had an opportunity to add to their lead in the fifth inning when Hosmer led off with a double into the right-field corner. Unlike the Royals have done throughout this postseason, though, they didn't play small ball to advance Hosmer. Moustakas popped out to the shortstop, Infante struck out, and Perez popped out to second.

The Royals now face Giants ace Madison Bumgarner in Game 5 before returning for Game 6 and possibly Game 7 at Kauffman Stadium. Yost and his guys aren't ready to throw in the towel just yet in spite of Saturday's blowout.

"I always feel good with this group. They've been playing great baseball," Yost said. "We got our tails whipped today, but it's Game 4 of the World Series. We're tied 2–2. How much more fun can that be? There is nothing better in the world. I've never felt so good about getting my tail whooped in my life because I'm sitting here thinking it's Game 4. It's tied 2–2. This is a phenomenal series. It's exciting, it's fun, and we've got another great game tomorrow that we get to play." ■

Bumgarner's Gem

Giants' Ace Puts San Francisco Up 3-2

James Shields needed to bounce back and pitch his best game of the postseason. For all intents and purposes, he did what he needed to do to win.

The Royals knew beating Giants' ace Madison Bumgarner would be a tall order, even with Shields, and not just because Bumgarner cruised to a win in Game 1 of this World Series against Shields. Bumgarner, despite not getting the national attention until now, has proven to be one of the best pitchers in World Series history.

Unfortunately for the Royals and their hopes of heading home with a 3 games to 2 lead in the World Series, Bumgarner cemented his name alongside the game's greats with a complete-game 5–0 shutout of Kansas City at AT&T Park, giving San Francisco that 3 games to 2 lead in the World Series.

"He was fantastic again," Royals manager Ned Yost said of Bumgarner's dominance. "You know what he does so well and what he's so impressive doing, he commands his fastball in and out, up and down. He commands his breaking ball in and out, and really can command that pitch down and away in the dirt when he wants to to get a strike. A lot of guys have trouble commanding that pitch; they'll hang it. A lot of guys have trouble just hitting that right spot where it just barely bounces where they can get that swing and miss. But boy, he sure had command of that tonight, too."

For a moment there, one halfway expected Bumgarner to hit a home run for the Giants, save someone from drowning in McCovey Cove, and then maybe end the night by delivering a baby. After all, in getting his second win against the Royals during this series, Bumgarner gave up only four hits and didn't walk any as his ERA in the World Series dropped to 0.56 and 1.13 in this postseason. In three World Series—2010, '12, and '14—Bumgarner upped his record to 4–0 with a 0.29 ERA in four starts.

As he did in Game 1, Bumgarner made most of the Royals batters look overmatched. When Kansas City managed to get a runner on base, Bumgarner seemed to go into a different mode. Six of his eight strikeouts came immediately after Kansas City got a hit. In the first inning, Lorenzo Cain blooped a two-out single to center. The next batter, Eric Hosmer, struck out on four pitches. The next inning, Salvador Perez led off with a base hit to right. Bumgarner proceeded to strike out the side: Mike Moustakas, Omar Infante, and Jarrod Dyson. Infante and Dyson whiffed on three pitches each. In the fifth, after Infante doubled with one out, Bumgarner struck out Dyson and Shields.

"He commanded all of his pitches and when you

thought you knew something, he did the exact opposite," said Moustakas, who went hitless in three at-bats. "That's what makes him good right now. He was throwing his fastball in there for strikes and his slider was sweeping all the way across the zone."

Shields, who was rocked for five runs and seven hits in three innings against the Giants in Game 1 and had only one appearance in this postseason of more than five innings, pitched as well against San Francisco this time around as he did in a win against the Los Angeles Angels three weeks earlier in the ALDS. Shields gave up two runs on eight hits. He struck out four and walked only one in six innings.

"I felt good, I felt like my stuff was there and I made my pitches when I needed to and unfortunately they found some holes," said Shields, a free agent after the season who might've been making his last start in a Royals uniform. "They probably had one hard-hit ball all night and that was the Hunter Pence deep fly ball. They didn't hit the ball hard, they just found a lot of holes and they did what they needed to do to win."

Shields got some help on that Pence fly to the deepest part of the park in the fifth. The Giants, leading 2–0 at that point, had runners at first and second with one out. Shields struck out Pablo Sandoval before Pence drove Shields' first pitch toward the gap in right-center before Cain, who played right field for each of the games in San Francisco, chased it down at the wall, near the 421 mark.

"That was a great play. That was a phenomenal play," Yost said. "That ball kept carrying and Cain just kept get-

ting after it and made another phenomenal play."

Pence scored the first run of the game—the only one the Giants needed—in the bottom of the second inning. After leading off the inning with a base hit, Pence eventually was at third with one out when Brandon Crawford grounded out to Infante, scoring Pence.

The Giants broke the game open in the bottom of the eighth when they scored two runs off Kelvin Herrera and one against Wade Davis.

The Royals headed home facing elimination with Game 6 on Tuesday night.

"You know what, we're going back to our home crowd. The place is going to be absolutely crazy," Yost said. "We feel good about our matchups. We've got to walk the tightrope now without a net, but our guys aren't afraid of walking the tightrope without a net. We fall off and we're dead. But we win Tuesday, nobody's got a net. It's going to be winner take all. So we think it's going to be fun." ■

Giants first baseman Brandon Belt tagged Royals catcher Salvador Perez out at first off his one hit in Game 5. (AP Images)

October 28, 2014 • Royals 10, Giants 0

Happy Homecoming

Royals Score 7 In Second Inning, Ventura Dominates Giants to Force Game 7

Perhaps fans should start calling Royals manager Ned Yost "Yostradamus" after the way things played out for Kansas City during the last couple games of the World Series. Yost has commented several times about how, deep down, he'd been hoping for this World Series to go seven games. He also showed unwavering confidence in his club after Madison Bumgarner and the Giants forced the Royals into an elimination Game 6.

Well, Yostradamus, you were correct. In front of another rambunctious Kauffman Stadium crowd, the Royals made beating the Giants look easy in a 10–0 win in Game 6, bringing about Wednesday night's Game 7— a winner-take-all end to the major league season.

"I've never felt more strongly about us winning a ballgame in my life than I did [Monday] on this game," Yost said. "I don't know why. It's just the confidence I have in these guys, because when you go in that locker room, you see the confidence they have in themselves. I just felt that we were going to win this game and get to Game 7 and see where that takes us. It's a good feeling. I didn't expect to win the game 10–0. I thought we'd squeak it out, but we're going to Game 7. That's all that matters."

The way they got through the Giants in Game 6 may matter. Behind another strong pitching performance from rookie Yordano Ventura, the Royals put the game out of reach with a seven-run second inning. Mike Moustakas gave Kansas City the lead with a double off starter Jake Peavy just inside the first-base bag that scored Alex Gordon, who led off the inning with a single and moved to third on a base hit by Salvador Perez. After Omar Infante struck out with runners at second and third, Alcides Escobar turned in the play of the game. He knocked a slow roller toward first. Giants first baseman Brandon Belt fielded the ball but hesitated, making sure Perez wasn't headed home. By the time Belt decided to make the play at first, Escobar had scooted by him and slid safely, feet first, into the bag. Nori Aoki then ripped an RBI single to left that gave Kansas City a 2–0 lead and ended Peavy's night.

"Esky's a real instinctual player," Yost said. "And his instincts come into play in plays like that. Those are plays that you can't really think about. It's just your instincts that allow you to do that."

After Lorenzo Cain lifted a soft two-run single to center off relief pitcher Yusmeiro Petit and then went to second on a wild pitch by Petit, the Giants brought

Yordano Ventura pitched seven shutout innings in the Royals' dominant 10–0 win in Game 6. (AP Images)

their infield in, trying to hold Kansas City at 4–0. It didn't work. Eric Hosmer bounced the ball in front of the plate and the towering chopper went over short-stop Brandon Crawford's head and into center field for a two-RBI double. That was Hosmer's 20th hit of the postseason, which tied him with Willie Wilson for most in a single postseason by a Royals player. The Royals put the dot on their exclamation point in the second when Billy Butler, who didn't start any of the games in San Francisco, doubled to center, scoring Hosmer and giving Kansas City a 7–0 lead.

The Giants threatened to get on the scoreboard in the half-inning after going down by seven. Ventura, following the long layoff of his teammates' offensive explosion, walked the bases loaded with one out before All-Star Buster Posey grounded into an inning-ending double play to Escobar. That was the only time the Giants had a runner at third base.

Otherwise, Ventura, who dedicated the game to his friend Oscar Taveras, the St. Louis Cardinals player who died in a car accident two days earlier, cruised very business-like through the Giants order. Ventura gave up three hits and five walks in seven innings. The performance gave Ventura the first postseason win of his career.

"You've got a 23-year-old kid pitching the biggest game that this stadium has seen in 29 years with our backs against the wall, and he goes out there in complete command of his emotions with great stuff, and throws seven shutout innings," Yost said. "I mean, we've talked all along about how special he is, but this just shows. You can't on a bigger stage than he was on tonight. To perform the way that he did was just special."

The Royals didn't let up, scoring single runs in the third, fifth, and seventh innings en route to a 15-hit night. The final hit and run of the night for Kansas City came when Moustakas belted a lead-off home run to right in the seventh off Hunter Strickland. It was Moustakas' first World Series home run, and fifth in this postseason, breaking Willie Aikens' franchise record of four homers in a single postseason.

After the game, Aikens tweeted: "Congratulations to Mike Moustakas for breaking my postseason home run record for the Royals. Way to go Moose. Keep it up Brother."

With the win in Game 6 the Royals have now won 100 games in a season for the first time since 1980, their only other trip to the World Series besides '85.

"As kids, what I fall back on is when I was 10 years old, hitting rocks in the backyard, trying to hit it over the fence for a home run. I never one time thought, okay, bases loaded, two out, bottom of the ninth, Game 5 of the World Series, you know? Never. It was always two outs, bottom of the ninth, Game 7 of the World Series, you know?" Yostradamus, er rather, Yost, said. "So it's special, you know? Secretly, yeah, you'd like to come in and win it in four, win it in five, but when this thing started, I really hoped we could play seven just for the experience of it and the thrill of it, and we're here now. So we feel good about our chances." ■

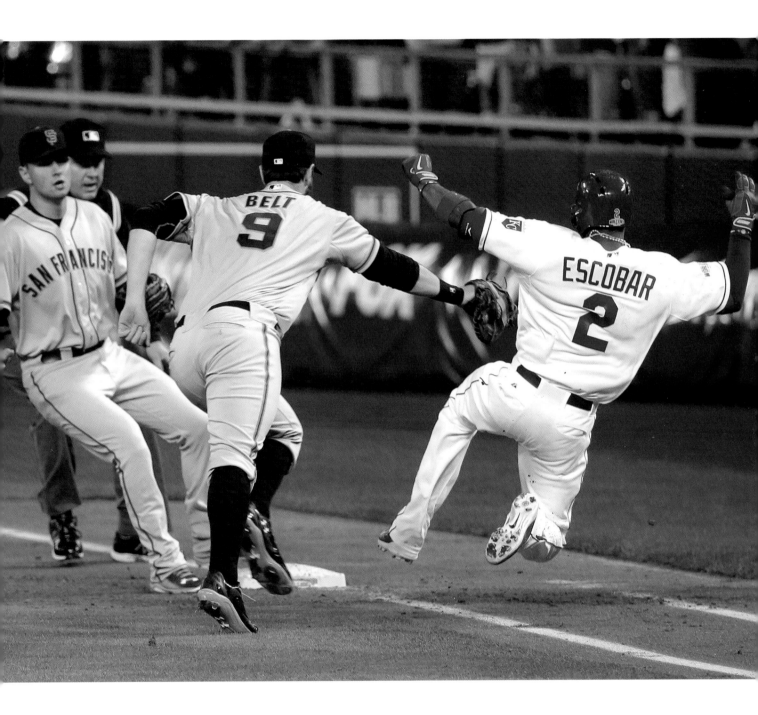

Alcides Escobar slides safely to first just out of Giants first baseman Brandon Belt's reach on an infield single. Escobar had a run, two hits, and an RBI in the Game 6 win. (AP Images)

October 29, 2014 • Giants 3, Royals 2

Ninety Feet Away

Bumgarner Stymies Royals Again, Strands Gordon at Third

Ninety feet. That's all that separated the Royals from pulling off the improbable in the same place where this crazy journey started 29 days ago. For a brief moment in late September, it would've been more plausible to find Elvis eating a North Town Burger at Chappell's than it would be to even imagine the Royals getting past the wild-card game, let alone reaching the World Series.

And yet, here they were, 90 feet—just 30 yards—from tying Game 7 with two outs in the bottom of the ninth inning with one of the greatest pitchers in World Series history facing the Royals player who had came up big in a similar spot 29 days earlier.

After a strikeout by Eric Hosmer and a foul out to first by Billy Butler, Alex Gordon, who had an RBI double in the second inning, stood at the plate against Giants ace Madison Bumgarner. Three days ago, Bumgarner mowed down the Royals for the second time in this World Series in a complete-game, four-hit shutout. Now he was one out from getting a five-inning save while allowing no runs and only one hit.

Gordon kept Kansas City's hopes alive, though, as he lined Bumgarner's 87 mph slider to left-center field. Centerfielder Gregor Blanco misplayed the ball, and it rolled to the wall. Left fielder Juan Perez had trouble grabbing the ball, which allowed Gordon to motor to third base. In the aftermath some fans wished third-base coach Mike Jirschele would've sent Gordon home. (Even an average throw from shortstop Brandon Crawford likely would've nailed Gordon by 27 feet for the final out of the Series.) Others claim that had Gordon charged hard out of the box on contact, he might've been able to score easily. Either way, he stood at third with two outs and Salvador Perez at the plate.

Salvy was hitless in the game, though he'd been plunked above the knee by starting pitcher Tim Hudson in the second inning. Going by averages, Perez was one of the guys the Royals would want at the plate in this situation. He was tied with Butler for the highest batting average on the team in the World Series at .333. And let's not forget that 29 days earlier, after looking silly in five previous at-bats, Perez propelled the Royals past Oakland in the wild-card game with a walk-off RBI single in the 12th inning.

But that hit was against Jason Hammel. To tie up Game 7, Perez would have to get a hit off Bumgarner. Whereas Hammel went low and away to Perez in the wild-card game, Bumgarner decided to throw high fastballs, which are the easiest to see and hardest to hit. Bumgarner threw six pitches—all fastballs—to Perez. Perez popped

Alex Gordon reaches third base after his line drive with two outs in the ninth inning got past Giants center fielder Gregor Blanco. Gordon, who represented the tying run, was stranded on third base when Salvador Perez popped up to end the game. (AP Images)

the last one up in foul territory near the Giants dugout at third base. Pablo Sandoval camped under it and made the catch. The Giants won Game 7, 3–2, having recorded their third World Series title in five years.

The Royals ended the game with a man at third.

"As magical as our run has been, to end up losing the ballgame by 90 feet is tough," Royals manager Ned Yost said. "But the hard part about this is that you work all year to climb to the top of the mountain, and then—boom—you fall back and you've got to start right back at the bottom again next year.

"But we've gained a ton of experience. I don't think I've ever been as proud of anything in my life as I have been of this team and the way they performed this post-season. It was just fantastic."

The Royals were their typically resilient selves in Game 7. After the Giants scored two against starter Jeremy Guthrie in the top of the second, Butler led off the inning with a single before Gordon, who batted .185 in the series, knocked a double to center that scored Butler from first. After Hudson hit Perez with a pitch and Mike Moustakas advanced Gordon to third with a fly out to left, the Royals tied the game at 2–2 on a sacrifice fly to center by Omar Infante.

Making his second appearance in this World Series and second ever in the Fall Classic, Guthrie gave up four hits and three runs in 3⅓ innings. With this being the last game of the season, each manager said his starting pitcher would be on a short leash. Giants manager Bruce Bochy went to his bullpen with two outs in the second and brought in former Royals pitcher Jeremy Affeldt. With one out in the fourth and runners at the corners in a 2–2 game, Yost brought in Kelvin Herrera. Designated hitter Michael Morse fought off a Herrera fastball and lined it to right, scoring Sandoval, who led off the inning with a hit.

Alex Gordon hits a double to drive in Billy Butler in the second inning. Gordon had two of the Royals' six hits in Game 7. (AP Images)

"We had the matchup we wanted with Morse and Herrera, and Morse did a great job of kind of just fighting off a high fastball and dumping it out into right field for the winning run," Yost said. "But Herrera was great...and Jeremy Guthrie was really throwing the ball well, too."

Morse's RBI hit made up Bochy's mind. Affeldt pitched another inning before Bochy plucked Bumgarner from the bullpen to start the fifth. Infante greeted him with a single, but that was the only base runner the Royals would have until Gordon reached in the ninth.

For his five innings of work, Bumgarner got the save while Affeldt was the game's winning pitcher. Bumgarner, who was selected as the World Series MVP after winning two games and saving one, saw his ERA for the World Series drop to 0.43.

Wade Davis and Greg Holland closed out the game for the Royals. As they'd done throughout the World Series, neither pitcher allowed a run. Both ended the series with a 0.00 ERA.

And just like that, this incredible month-long ride for the Royals was over. Through the improbable post-season run, which came 29 years after their last one, the Royals gained fans across the country and certainly brought the Kansas City community together unlike any other sports team, personality, or politician had ever done.

Just like they did after winning the ALCS, Hosmer and several of his teammates went to the Power & Light District as a way to thank the fans. A rally honoring the team was held at Kauffman Stadium the morning after Game 7.

"On a scale of one to 10 in terms of support through the postseason, it's got to be 14," Yost said. "It was phenomenal. What our fans did and the excitement in the city here for this last month, it's just been absolutely unbelievable." ∎

Thousands of Royals fans came out to Kauffman Stadium the morning after Game 7 to show their support for the 2014 Royals, the first Royals team to reach the World Series since 1985. (AP Images)

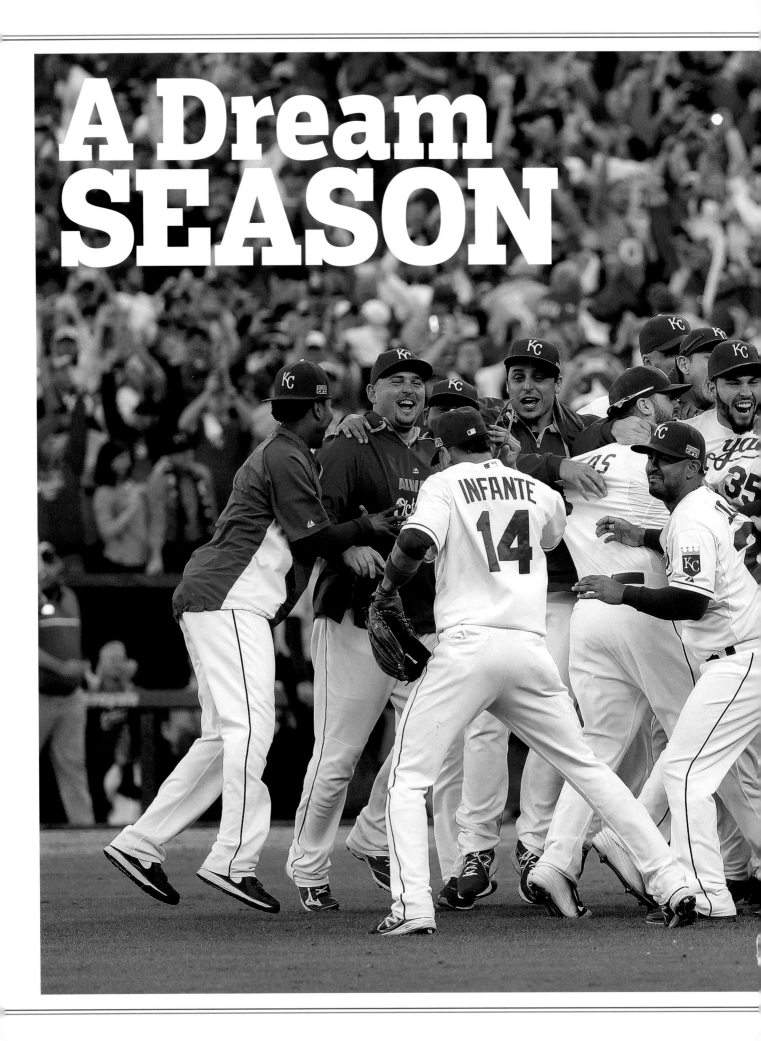

A Dream SEASON

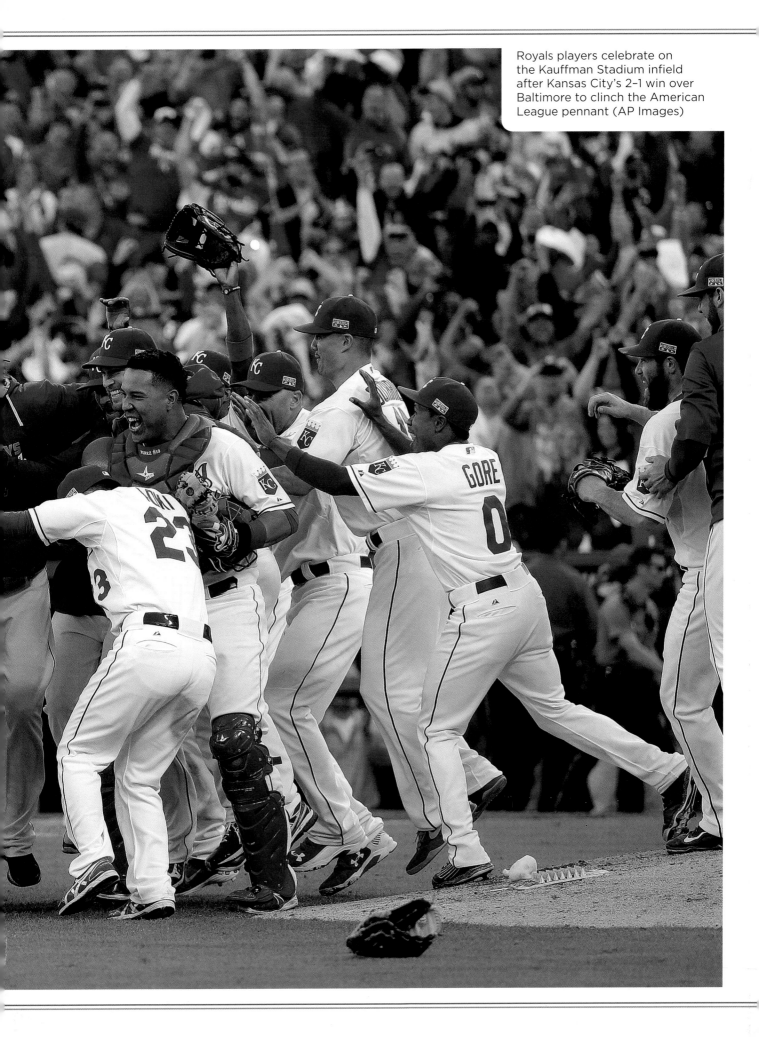

Royals players celebrate on the Kauffman Stadium infield after Kansas City's 2–1 win over Baltimore to clinch the American League pennant (AP Images)

Back on Top

During June Hot Streak, Royals Claim First Place

On August 29, 2003, the Royals were in first place in the division, one game ahead of the Chicago White Sox. Billy Butler was beginning his junior year at Wolfson High School in Jacksonville, Florida. Alex Gordon was a freshman at the University of Nebraska. Mike Moustakas was about to start his freshman year, too...at Chatsworth High School in California. Eric Hosmer was in the eighth grade. That's the last time the Royals were in first place that late in the season.

That is...until the club took over first place in the AL Central with an 11–4 win at Detroit on June 17, 2014.

"It's fleeting," Royals manager Ned Yost cautioned. "It can leave tomorrow. You've got to stay on top of your game."

The Royals certainly were on top of their game at the time. The win, which gave the Royals a half-game lead over Detroit, marked the club's ninth in a row and 10th of their previous 11. When the winning streak began with an 8–4 victory against the New York Yankees, the Royals were tied with the Minnesota Twins for last in the division, five games behind Detroit.

Things were going so well for the Royals when they leapfrogged the Tigers that they had little trouble with reigning Cy Young champ Max Scherzer. Kansas City tagged Scherzer for a career-high 10 runs in four-plus innings. Gordon and Moustakas each hit a two-run

homer during a seven-hit, seven-run second inning.

After Butler led off the inning with a double, Gordon launched a 414-foot home run to right field, which gave Kansas City a 2–0 advantage. Then, following a walk to Salvador Perez, Moustakas also homered to right. The Tigers didn't record an out until Hosmer, the ninth batter of the inning, grounded back to Scherzer. The Royals scored their seventh run of the inning on that play, as Nori Aoki, who had singled earlier, crossed the plate.

"Anytime you can do that to a starting pitcher in the second inning, you know they're going to be frustrated a little bit," Gordon said.

Yordano Ventura gave up eight hits and three runs in seven innings of work. He evened his record at 5–5 with the win. Although he gave up two runs in the second, Ventura's only trouble inning was the fifth with Kansas City leading 10–2. Detroit loaded the bases with one out and then, after Ian Kinsler flew out, Ventura walked Miguel Cabrera, which made it a 10–3 game. Ahead in the count 0–2 to Victor Martinez, Ventura flew a fastball to the backstop. With Ventura's velocity and the Royals' good fortune, the ball hit something hard on the backstop and jetted back toward catcher Perez. By that time the runner at third, Eugenio Suarez, was stuck between home and third. He tried to scamper back to third, but Perez threw a strike to Moustakas and

got Suarez for the final out.

"The ball went past Salvy, and I saw it shoot back to him so I shot over to third just in case he throws it," Moustakas said. "And he threw it—a great play and we were able to get [Suarez] out."

Kansas City won its next game against Detroit, on June 18, and moved one-and-a half games ahead of the Tigers. In that 2–1 win—the 10th straight—the Royals scored their first run when Gordon grounded a ball up the middle in the first inning, and it took a funny bounce off second base, allowing Hosmer to score.

That's the way the bounces seemed to go for the Royals during much of the 2014 season. That's the way things seem to go for teams during a championship season.

Although they were in first place in late August 2003, the Royals ended up finishing third in the division with a record of 83–79. It was the last time they finished above .500 until 2013's 86–76 mark. Of course, with their 38–32 record in mid-June, the 2014 season was still 11 days from the midway point.

"What's the date?" Yost said. "It's nice, but we've got a lot of games to play. We don't get all geeked up. We're on a nice run right now. We'll just keep it going. It's better than the alternative; trust me." ■

The Royals won 17 of 27 games in June, including a streak of 10 straight, which allowed them to climb back to the top of the American League Central with a win over the Tigers on June 17. (AP Images)

4
OF
ALEX GORDON

Former Prized Prospect at Third Base Strikes Gold in the Outfield

The play stood out to Alex Gordon. Late in the 2012 season—September 26 to be exact—the Royals were in Detroit. Miguel Cabrera, perhaps the best hitter of this generation, was in the hunt for baseball's elusive Triple Crown.

Leading off the fifth inning of a 4–4 game, Cabrera launched a moon shot to left against Jeremy Guthrie. Gordon raced back to the wall and stood there, as if watching it leave. Suddenly, as the ball returned to Earth, Gordon jumped up and robbed Cabrera of the home run.

"I'm always a big fan of robbing home runs and I think I did it twice this year," Gordon said after that season. "Miguel Cabrera's was pretty cool."

He didn't rob anyone of home runs during the 2014 American League playoffs, but Gordon played outstanding defense in left, complete with at least one play that will go down in Royals postseason lore. Royals fans certainly appreciated it—even if it's become expected of Gordon during the past few seasons.

That play in Detroit at the end of the 2012 season was one of many that helped him win a Rawlings Gold Glove Award for the second consecutive season. Besides being the 20th Gold Glove Award in Royals history, Gordon's 2012 hardware gave him the distinction of being the first Royals player since Frank White in 1986–1987 to win the award in back-to-back seasons. Gordon repeated in 2013, becoming just the third Royals player—along with White and Amos Otis—to win the Gold Glove at least three times.

Perhaps as intriguing as winning it three times was the fact that Gordon won his first one in 2011. Gordon, early in his career as a third baseman, seemed destined for a career of mediocrity, at best, filled with time on the disabled list and a career full of fans second guessing the sanity of the Royals for selecting him with the second overall pick in the 2005 MLB Amateur Draft and tabbing him as "the next George Brett." Sure, he grew up in Nebraska as a big Royals fan and was an outstanding player at the University of Nebraska, but none of that meant a hill of beans early in his career.

After tearing things up at Double A Wichita in 2006 while playing for Frank White, Gordon came to the big leagues in 2007. He immediately looked like a high-strikeout player with a little pop in his bat who could commit close to 20 errors each season at third. That's assuming he'd be on the field. He was "officially" on the disabled list in three straight seasons.

Kansas City moved Alex Gordon to the outfield in 2010, a change that jumpstarted the former third baseman's career. (AP Images)

Everything changed during 2010 when the Royals decided to move Gordon to the outfield. He wasn't setting the world on fire, and their No. 1 draft pick of 2007, Mike Moustakas, was burning through Double A pitching and appeared to be the third baseman of the future. So, Gordon, who was batting .194 at the time, was sent to Triple A Omaha in May, a month after returning from the DL, to start working with Rusty Kuntz, the Royals' current first-base coach who was a roving instructor at the time.

As expected for someone who had never played outfield, it took some time to learn the position. A lot of time. But his athleticism and natural instincts, along with Kuntz's tireless work, helped Gordon become a big league outfielder.

That move to the outfield has been fortuitous for both Gordon and the Royals. Besides the three Gold Gloves, Gordon has changed his physical preparation. As his younger brother Derek, who pitches for the Kansas City T-Bones, an independent professional team in Kansas City, says: "Nobody's going to out-work Alex—no way." Gordon's daily preparation, which starts at the stadium each day long before most of his teammates arrive, has become somewhat legendary.

That dedication has paid off. Gordon hasn't been on the disabled list since 2010, playing in at least 151 games in each of the last four seasons. As importantly, his offensive production has improved, and he's been selected as an American League All-Star each of the last two seasons.

"He's one of the best all-around players in the league," pitcher James Shields said during the ALCS. "He can do it all. He plays Gold Glove defense, he can hit for power, he can steal a base. He does everything well. It's really been a treat to be able to play with him."

With the emergence of Moustakas, Eric Hosmer, and Salvador Perez and the addition of players such as Shields, Lorenzo Cain, and Alcides Escobar, Gordon—a member of the old guard—has become a team leader. After all, he and Billy Butler are the two longest-tenured players on the club.

"I don't think it's me," he said of his poise after Game 1 of the ALCS, when he was the main cog in the Royals' win over Baltimore. "It's our team. We have a great chemistry in the clubhouse. We're all pulling for each other. And it's really a lot of fun right now." ■

Above: Alex Gordon earned a Gatorade bath, administered by catcher Salvador Perez, after he hit a two-run walk-off home run to beat the Minnesota Twins on August 26. Opposite: Gordon was instrumental in the Royals' 12-6 win over the Twins on August 17—their highest-scoring output of the month. He scored three runs. (AP Images)

Welcome Back, Zack

Cain, Escobar Help Defeat Ace They Were Traded For

After going on a 10-game winning streak that gave the Royals a one-and-a-half game cushion in the AL Central in mid-June, Kansas City lost its next four and fell two-and-half games behind Detroit. In order to stop the bleeding, the Royals would have to beat their former ace, Zack Greinke and the Los Angeles Dodgers.

Lost in the talk of the trade that brought James Shields and Wade Davis to Kansas City, is a trade that general manager Dayton Moore made almost exactly two years earlier. Perhaps it's because it occurred at a time when fans still expected the Royals to trade top players, and the trade with Tampa sent a top prospect. Regardless, the deal Moore made with the Milwaukee Brewers on December 19, 2010, could go down as one of the best in Royals history.

The Royals sent Greinke, the AL Cy Young winner in 2009, along with Yuniesky Betancourt, to the Brewers in exchange for outfielder Lorenzo Cain, shortstop Alcides Escobar, and pitchers Jeremy Jeffress and Jake Odorizzi. (Besides the great players Cain and Escobar have become for the Royals, Odorizzi was a component in the trade with the Rays that brought Shields and Davis to Kansas City.)

Greinke, who had faced the Royals twice before while pitching for Milwaukee and the Los Angeles Angels, got off to a hot start in 2014, winning his first five decisions,

losing one, and then winning his next two. By the end of June, when the ultra-talented Dodgers visited Kauffman Stadium for the first meeting between the two clubs since 2005, Greinke was 9–3 with a 2.57 ERA.

That didn't seem to matter to the Royals, who had a shuffled lineup and went on to win 5–3 on June 23. Manager Ned Yost kept Cain in the leadoff spot for the second straight game but moved Omar Infante from second to the sixth sport, moved Eric Hosmer to the No. 2 hole, followed by Billy Butler, Alex Gordon, Salvador Perez, Infante, Mike Moustakas, Escobar, and Jarrod Dyson.

The revised lineup must've worked, as Kansas City tagged Greinke for a season-high five runs and 11 hits in five and two-third innings. Perez led off the Royals half of the second with a 415-foot home run to left, giving Kansas City a 1–0 lead. Later in the inning, with two outs, Escobar singled, moved to second on a wild pitch, and then scored on a base hit by Dyson.

The Royals extended their lead in the fifth when Dyson, who went 3-for-3 with two RBIs, led off with a single and was driven in by Cain. Kansas City got two insurance runs the next inning when Escobar tripled with two outs, scoring Perez, who'd led off the inning with a double. Up next, Dyson singled and knocked in Escobar and knocked out Greinke.

"The fastball was good but really bad off-speed.

That was the problem today," Greinke said after the game. "They didn't have to respect it. It was like I did them a favor when I threw off-speed."

That was all the Royals needed behind a strong pitching performance by Jeremy Guthrie, who won two games during the 10-game winning streak and hadn't lost since the game before that streak. Guthrie gave up two runs and seven hits over seven and two-third innings. He improved to 5–6. Greg Holland gave up a home run in the ninth to Adrian Gonzalez but picked up his 22nd save of the season.

The Royals' return on the Greinke trade turned out well this night. Cain, who led off, had two hits and one RBI. Escobar, who was batting eighth, had two hits and scored twice.

"The guys that got traded for me are playing good, and I think even the Odorizzi guy is pitching good, too," said Greinke. "It looks like they got some good players." ■

Former Royals ace Zack Greinke was no match for his previous team on June 23. Greinke allowed a season-high five runs and 11 hits in five and two-third innings to the Royals in Kansas City's 5–3 win over Greinke's Dodgers. (AP Images)

40, 17, 56

P

KELVIN HERRERA, WADE DAVIS & GREG HOLLAND

Three-Headed Monster: Trio of K.C. Relievers Shut Down Opponents

Royals general manager Dayton Moore and manager Ned Yost have known that they're not going to build a championship-caliber team by trying to find a bunch of sluggers. Especially in a ballpark like Kauffman Stadium. It's going to take speed, solid defense, and, of course, pitching.

During the 2012 and '13 seasons, the Royals' Pitcher of the Year ended up being the team's closer, Greg Holland. And with good reason. In Holland, the Royals enjoyed, frankly, a luxury item they didn't really need: a dominant closer. Oh, sure, they were in the wild-card chase in 2013, but they didn't really need Holland's dominance. For the most part, he wasn't closing meaningful games. He was about as overpowering as possible, though, saving a club-record 47 games with a 1.21 ERA in 68 appearances in 2013. Although Jonathan Broxton was the main closer early in '12 and saved 23 of the club's 72 wins that year, Holland emerged as the future. He saved 16 games and won seven, which was third highest win total on the team that season.

With Moore's long-held belief that pitching is a huge commodity in baseball and the fact that the Royals would have to manufacture some wins, Yost began to realize during the 2014 spring training what type of arms he had in his bullpen in front of Holland—namely Kelvin Herrera and Luke Hochevar.

With his flat-billed hat cocked to one side, it's easy to recognize Herrera, who signed with the Royals as an undrafted free agent after a tryout in the Dominican Republic in December 2006. If you don't recognize his signature cap, just look for the pitcher who tips the radar gun past 100 with his fastball and has a 90-mile-per-hour change-up with movement. Heading into 2014, Herrera had appeared in 79 games for the Royals since 2011.

Hochevar doesn't have the electric stuff of Herrera, but after five less-than-stellar years in the rotation, Hochevar, the club's first-round pick (first overall) in 2006, found his niche in the bullpen in 2013 as the

Royals relievers Kelvin Herrera, Wade Davis, and Greg Holland each finished the 2014 regular season with ERAs of less than 2.00—1.41, 1.00, and 1.44 respectively. Davis (opposite) surpassed his career mark of 3.91 by nearly three runs. (AP Images)

set-up guy. His ERA went from 5.73 as a starter in 2011 to 1.92 as a reliever in '12, and his strikeout-to-walk ratio between the two seasons went from 144–61 to 82–17, a marked difference. Early in spring training of 2014, though, Hochevar felt something wrong in his elbow. An MRI determined the Royals' and Hochevar's worst fear: Tommy John surgery. Just when things were looking up, his season was done before it started.

As a last resort, the Royals moved Wade Davis into Hochevar's spot. Davis seemed to be the "throwaway," if you will, in the blockbuster trade in December 2012 that brought James Shields to Kansas City and sent, among other young players, Wil Myers to Tampa Bay. After struggling through performance issues on the field and the death of his stepbrother, 2013 wasn't a spectacular year for Davis. His 8–11 record and 5.32 ERA will attest to that.

But much like Hochevar a year earlier, Davis found his niche. Since moving to the bullpen full-time in 2014, Davis, who's reserved and seemingly all business when he's on the mound, has been nearly unhittable throughout the regular season and American League playoffs.

Early in the season, Yost, who's received plenty of criticism for moves he's made or not made during his time in Kansas City, realized he had a dependable three-headed monster with three dominant one-inning pitchers and he re-invented how to manage the bullpen late in the game. Herrera became the seventh-inning pitcher, Davis came in the eighth, and then Holland closed it. If the Royals hit the seventh inning of a game with a lead, they were in good shape.

Who are we kidding? They were nearly unbeatable. When leading after six innings this year, the Royals were 68–4. If they had a lead an inning later, they were 75–1.

"Baseball is not a game of perfection," Hall of Fame broadcaster Denny Matthews says, "but those three have been as close to perfect as you can get."

The three relievers combined to give up just three home runs during the regular season. Herrera, who finished the 2014 regular season with a 4–3 record and 1.41 ERA in 70 games, had a scoreless streak that spanned 30 appearances. Davis didn't allow a run for 20 consecutive appearances and didn't allow an extra-base hit for 43 straight appearances. Then there's Holland, a two-time All Star, who saved 46 games with a 1.44 ERA in 2014. During the last two months of the season—after the trade deadline—the three pitchers combined for a 0.86 ERA in 73 innings.

Then there was the postseason. Herrera pitched in seven of the eight Royals' American League playoff games and allowed six hits and one earned run for a 1.08 ERA. Davis appeared in all eight AL games and went 2–0. Holland saved six games, including all four in the ALCS, in eight appearances with a miniscule 1.13 ERA.

He rounds out a spectacular bullpen.

"Our offense has a lot of confidence in everybody we've got down there," Yost said. "If we can take a lead and get it to the bullpen, odds are we're going to be celebrating a victory at the end of the day."

By the way, for the superstitious types or anyone looking for a sign during the 2014 postseason that this could be the Royals' year, check this out. Royals pitcher Bret Saberhagen, who was the MVP of the 1985 World Series, spent time at the hospital during that World Series as his wife at the time gave birth to their first son, Drew. A few years ago, Drew, who was a college baseball player, transferred from Pepperdine to Western Carolina. One of his teammates was Greg Holland. Taking that a step further: between the wild-card game and the start of the ALDS in Anaheim, Holland went home to North Carolina for the birth of his son. (Cue Rod Serling and The Twilight Zone theme.) ∎

Relief pitcher Greg Holland carries the flag after the Royals beat the Athletics 9–8 in the American League wild card game. (AP Images)

DAYTON MOORE & NED YOST

World Series Marks Career Pinnacle for Royals Leaders

What a difference a year makes. Or seven or eight.

Royals general manager Dayton Moore, a baseball man from the days before he could even think about becoming a man, desired to cultivate the Royals into winners more than you can imagine. That's been the case since he became the club's sixth general manager on June 8, 2006. Developing a winner, though, takes time—especially with how depleted the Royals farm system was when Moore took over.

And it certainly took time. In Moore's seventh full season, 2013, the Royals finished 86–76. It was the club's first winning season since 2003 and the most number of victories since winning 92 in 1989. Even though the Royals were in the chase for a wild-card berth until the last week of the season, they fell short and finished third in the AL Central, seven games behind Detroit.

Key players on the 2013 roster were homegrown, including Billy Butler and Alex Gordon—both of whom were selected by GM Allard Baird—Greg Holland (10th round, 2007), Eric Hosmer (first round, 2008), Mike Moustakas (first round, 2007), and Salvador Perez (non-drafted free agent signing, 2006).

After the winning record and wild-card push in 2013, many fans remained unhappy and sought more progress. Still, he felt there was reason to look ahead optimistically to 2014.

"I believe that all our players that are signed long-term or under team control are going to get better," he said during his 2013 postseason press conference. "Is it just going to happen? No. They are going to have to continue to work hard, apply instructions, and make adjustments. They are going to have to continue to commit to becoming great players."

Winning never comes easy. But decades of losing can do funny things to a fan base, whether that fan base is old enough to remember the "glory days" of the 1970s and '80s or young enough to be part of today's society of instant gratification. So, after enduring losing season after losing season and bad trade after bad acquisition under previous general managers, seven seasons of waiting for "the process" to work was an eternity.

Sending Zack Greinke to Milwaukee for (mainly) a light-hitting shortstop named Alcides Escobar and an outfielder named Lorenzo Cain, who had played a whopping 43 games in the big leagues in six professional seasons? And then you're going to trade the future greatest

Kansas City general manager Dayton Moore needed time to rebuild the team after he took the helm in June 2006, but patience has paid off for Royals fans, who enjoyed the team's first winning season in a decade in 2013 and its first playoff appearance since 1985 in 2014. (AP Images)

Royal ever, Wil Myers, along with two stud minor-league pitchers for a short-term starter in James Shields and a barely-average starter named Wade Davis?

Are you serious?

Those moves, though, turned out to be quite deft and have more than vindicated Moore.

Critics also questioned Moore for backing Ned Yost, whom he'd hired in May 2010 to lead this club. Yost was Moore's guy, who he knew well from their days in the Atlanta Braves organization. Moore was scouting or in the front office from 1994–2006 while Yost coached in various capacities from 1991–2002.

Throughout 2013 and '14, in particular, Royals fans came up with all sorts of words to describe Yost, and most of them aren't very pleasant.

He's unapologetic. He comes off as condescending. And he's made moves that fans and former players alike think are boneheaded, which has fostered the term "Yosted" to describe anything and everything negative in life.

It was a controversial decision Yost made in the sixth inning of the wild-card game that almost kept the Royals from advancing in the 2014 playoffs. After starter Shields gave up a bloop single and then issued a walk with two on and nobody out and Kansas City holding a 3–2 lead with Brandon Moss—who homered earlier—coming to the plate, Yost pulled Shields, who'd thrown 88 pitches, and brought in starter Yordano Ventura. Moss launched Ventura's third pitch 432 feet to dead center. It seemed as though social media might combust at once with thousands of fans and other detractors saying how the Royals had been "Yosted." Funny, though. The Royals overcame any questionable judgment decisions in that first postseason game and went on to make 2014 the "Yostseason."

That Yostseason should've caused the doubters to eat crow, but the negative perceptions mean little to the Royals manager.

"I don't need vindication," Yost said after the Royals swept the Orioles in the ALCS. "I'm comfortable with who I am. And everything that I look at, I don't look at much. But I'm the dumbest guy on the face of the earth. But I know that's not true…I am smart enough to hire really, really good coaches and use them. But I'm real comfortable in my own skin. I don't feel like I need vindication. I'm not looking for it, don't care for it.

"My whole goal—none of this was ever about me. To win a championship was all about this city, our fans and these players. I've been there six times before, I know how special it is. And I wanted my players to experience it. I wanted the city of Kansas City to experience it and our fans."

And, thanks to Dayton Moore, who built a deep farm system and assembled a club with pitching and speed that could win at spacious Kauffman Stadium, Yost was able to take that group of players, push the right buttons, use each player to his strength, foster a cohesive locker room, and lead them to the World Series for the first time in their careers and only the third time in Royals franchise history, en route to becoming the first manager ever to win his first eight postseason games as a skipper.

"These kids, from the minute you saw them you knew they were going to be special," Yost said after winning the AL championship. "Then they won championships in A ball together and they won championships in Double A together and they won championships in Triple A together. And then their goal was to get up here and win a championship, and today they accomplished that." ∎

Royals fans took a while to warm to manager Ned Yost, whom Moore hired in 2010. But Nost's decision-making through the 2014 postseason, now referred to as the "Yostseason," took the Royals to their first World Series in nearly 30 years. (AP Images)

Fateful Fan

Devoted South Korean Fan Provides Good Luck During Incredible Journey

Adding to the craziness of the 2014 season and the idea of things happening for a reason, a man named SungWoo Lee traveled more than 6,500 miles (one way) to see the Royals in person for the first time.

There's no way anyone could've anticipated what would transpire during the 10-day voyage.

SungWoo Lee's love of the Royals began 20 years ago. He was trying to improve his English by watching Major League Baseball games and he saw a broadcast of a Royals game from Kauffman Stadium. After Royals batter Jeff King launched a home run, the South Korean immediately fell in love with the "beautiful K" and wanted to learn all he could about the Royals. He would get up at 3:00 in the morning to watch the Royals play a day game or he would wait until well after dinner to see a night game. He quickly became the Royals' biggest fan in Korea—heck, possibly the Royals' biggest fan outside of Kansas City.

After conversing with fellow Royals fans through Twitter (@KoreanFan_KC) for three years, the 38-year-old SungWoo finally made plans to visit Kansas City in August. As his Royals friends in Kansas City caught wind, the entire city—fans, politicians, the media, former Royals, and the Royals organization—stepped up and allowed SungWoo to fulfill a fantasy experience for any Royals fan.

As part of SungWoo's trip, he...

- Took a tour of the Negro Leagues Baseball Museum with the director of the museum, Bob Kendrick
- Ate lunch at Arthur Bryant's
- Was interviewed by local media
- Was featured in articles on Deadspin and *USA TODAY*
- Got an email from Mike Sweeney
- Received a tour of Kauffman Stadium from Jennifer Splittorff, the daughter of the late Royals Hall of Fame pitcher Paul Splittorff
- Visited the Double A team, the Northwest Arkansas Naturals, and shook hands with each player in the clubhouse
- Received a personalized Royals jersey from the team
- Received a personalized Chiefs jersey from the Chiefs
- Was featured on *SportsCenter*

SungWoo Lee shows off his "super fan" Royals cap before Game 1 of the World Series. SungWoo traveled 6,500 miles from South Korea in August to see the Royals in person for the first time. He returned to Kansas City in October for the World Series. (AP Images)

- Received an autographed Frank White jersey from White
- Received a pin from George Brett
- Threw out a first pitch at Kauffman Stadium
- Danced around with the W that Kauffman Stadium puts up after each victory

And something strange happened along the way. The Royals became the hottest team in baseball. Since being down by eight games in the AL Central on July 21 with a 48–50 record, the Royals went 9–3 in the games leading up to SungWoo's visit. When he arrived, though, on August 5, the Royals clobbered the Arizona Diamondbacks in Arizona 12–2. That was their second win in what became an eight-game winning streak. The Royals finished SungWoo's trip with an 8–1 record, and they were in first place in the division.

SungWoo returned to Kauffman Stadium to see Game 1 of the World Series. It seemed like a good luck charm and even destiny. After all, during his last excursion to Kauffman to watch his team, the Royals swept the San Francisco Giants. ■

SungWoo Lee shows off a World Series towel before Game 1 of the World Series at Kauffman Stadium. The World Series marked the South Korean fan's second trip to Kansas City in 2014. During his first visit in August, the Royals posted an 8-1 record and ascended to first place in the AL Central. (AP Images)

"That's What Speed Do"

Small Ball Ways Pace Royals' Offense

For a team that didn't have a lot of power, the 2014 Royals used a formula that worked for the Royals of the 1970s and '80s: great team speed, which applies to covering a ton of real estate in the outfield and, of course, causing havoc on the bases.

Their game at Kauffman Stadium on September 15 was a signature moment for that speed. After dropping three of four to Boston—five of their last seven overall—and seeing a half-game lead in the AL Central flip to a two-game deficit to Detroit, the Royals needed a revitalizing win. They got just that in unusual fashion against the Chicago White Sox.

After trailing Chicago 3–0 in the seventh, the Royals scored two and trailed 3–2, heading into the bottom of the ninth. With one out in the inning, Mike Moustakas, who'd been struggling at the plate, doubled. Jarrod Dyson, who coined the phrase "that's what speed do" a couple years ago, pinch ran for Moustakas. Moments later, after stealing third, Dyson scored on a wild pitch by Jake Petricka to tie the game.

Nori Aoki, Kansas City's hottest hitter at the time, doubled with two outs. Terrance Gore, a September call-up with blazing speed, ran for Aoki. The next batter, Lorenzo Cain, chopped an infield grounder. In a scene you'd expect from the movie *Major League,* Cain was safe at first as Gore sped home from second with the winning run.

"I was definitely going to be safe," Cain said. "I just put it in play and ran."

That could be the offensive mantra for the Royals in 2014: put the ball in play and run. They definitely weren't a long-ball threat as a team, finishing last in the majors with 95 home runs in 2014. It's only the 10th time in franchise history—dating back to 1969—and second time since 1982 that the club has hit fewer than 100 homers.

For this club to win, it would have to rely on good pitching and speed. As a side note, a couple days before that walk-off (or run-off) win against Chicago, manager Ned Yost tweaked the Royals lineup. He made the top of the order speed-heavy with Alcides Escobar leading off, Aoki batting second, and Cain third.

"[Escobar's] been really creating some scoring opportunities for us, getting on base. [He] and Nori both have done a great job kind of transforming the top of that order," Yost said. "Now if we can get a couple guys hot in the middle of the order, we're going to be okay."

And why not? The Royals finished the season with 153 stolen bases, which was most in the majors and happened to be the same number as last year. Since their first trip to the World Series in 1980, the Royals have eclipsed 150 stolen bases only five times: 1983 (182), 1989 (154), 1996 (195), and then the last two seasons. From 1975 through '80, though, with the likes of Amos Otis, Fred Patek, Frank White, and Willie Wilson, the

Outfielder Jarrod Dyson slides into third base after hitting a triple against Minnesota on August 15. Dyson led the 2014 Royals with 36 stolen bases. (AP Images)

Royals never had fewer than 150. And in three of those six years, Kansas City hitters swiped more than 200 bags. Guess what else from those six seasons? They won the Western Division four times: 1976, '77, '78, and '80.

Of course, that's not necessarily a formula for annually reaching the World Series, but it worked for the Royals during the regular season in 2014, and it carried over to the postseason. The Royals showed during the postseason that having speed on bases can cause havoc for defenses. And, speaking of defense, they showed during the postseason that Cain, Dyson, Alex Gordon, and Aoki have enough speed to cover the vast outfield at Kauffman Stadium or any other stadium for that matter.

"When you range as far as we range in the outfield," Yost said, "especially when these games are as tight as they are, you just feel like you're never going to get a break because our defensive guys are absolutely everywhere, and it is a bit deflating." ■

Opposite: Lorenzo Cain scores on a Billy Butler single during the first inning of Game 2 of the World Series. Above: Cain slides safely under the tag of Giants second baseman Joe Panik in Game 2. A key cog in the Royals' speed game, Cain stole 28 bases during the regular season. (AP Images)

16
DH

BILLY BUTLER

"Country Breakfast" Is a Natural at the Plate

A player doesn't forget his first major league game. Billy Butler definitely won't. It was May 1, 2007, against the Los Angeles Angels of Anaheim. Bartolo Colon, one of the American League's best pitchers at the time, was on the mound.

With a veteran's confidence, and not that of a recently-turned 21-year-old kid, Butler stepped calmly inside the batter's box for his first plate appearance. He got a hit.

"I was absolutely nervous, as you should be at that point in your career," said Butler, who went 2-for-4 that day. "I'm still nervous when I go up there. It's one of those things that hopefully never goes away. That's the edge, the fire inside, wanting to do well and help the team."

It was one debut that many fans couldn't wait for.

See, Billy Butler, who has one of the purest swings you'll ever see, was born to be a hitter. Shoot, colleges started contacting him when he was about 12 or 13. Butler, who was given the nickname "Country Breakfast" by some fans in 2011, eventually signed a letter of intent with one of those schools that contacted him early, the University of Florida. Of course the Royals interrupted those plans when the club selected him with the 14th overall pick in the 2004 draft.

It looked immediately as if the Royals got what they needed. Butler was the Rookie of the Year in the Pioneer League in 2004 and then the California League Rookie of the Year in '05. In 2006 he won the Texas League batting title with a .331 average. All of that was before he could legally drink.

"The thing I like about Billy is that he has always been a hitter, so he knows what he's doing," said Frank White, who managed Butler at Double A Wichita, Kansas in 2008. "Then you listen to his comments when he comes back to the dugout and you know he follows the sequence of pitches and what the pitchers are trying to do."

When Butler first made it to Wichita, during his second season of professional baseball, he was a typical young player trying so hard to continue advancing in the system. His youth and, frankly, immaturity would show up if he didn't like a call by an umpire or if he simply had a bad at-bat.

"Oh, Billy and I had a lot of conversations," White said with a laugh. "We'd talk about his body language,

Billy Butler, who has a career batting average of .295, is valued for his contributions at the plate. But his value was diverse in 2014; he stole a key base in the AL playoffs and saw his slugging percentage as a first baseman increase to .815. (AP Images)

for instance, when umpires would call a strike and how long it would take him to get back in the box between pitches. I tried to give him some ideas of what umpires in the big leagues think about rookies and the way players should ask questions about pitches instead of being so obvious about his displeasure for the pitch."

Then, White paused and thought for a minute about Butler before gushing.

"Really, he's just an awesome kid."

And, he's been a pretty good player.

In 2009 Butler became only the fifth player in major league history to record at least 50 doubles and 20 home runs in a season before turning 24 years old. He joined Hank Greenberg (1934), Alex Rodriguez (1996), Albert Pujols (2003), and Miguel Cabrera (2006), when he had 51 doubles and 21 homers—at the age of 23.

Then, in 2012, Butler was selected as the Silver Slugger Award winner at designated hitter in the American League. He was the seventh Royals player to win the award, joining George Brett (three times), Willie Wilson (twice), plus Hal McRae, White, Gary Gaetti, and Dean Palmer.

Through various acquisitions and signings, not to mention the emergence in 2011 of Eric Hosmer at first base, Butler has become, almost exclusively, the club's designated hitter. During 2011–13 he played in the field for a total of 38 games—all at first. In 2013 he appeared in all of the club's 162 games for the first time in his career.

Butler, who's the longest tenured Royals player, had a down season overall in 2014, batting a career-low .271 with nine home runs and 66 RBIs (the lowest number of homers and RBIs since his first and second year in the league, respectively). But he showed that he has value defensively. He was a key to keeping the Royals in a playoff hunt during August, when Hosmer missed a month with a hand injury. Butler played a solid first

base (two errors in 37 total games at first in '14) and saw his on-base plus slugging percentage increase from .646 as a designated hitter to .815 as a first baseman.

Although he's slow afoot—enough so that Toronto Blue Jays right fielder Jose Bautista threw him out at first in May of this season on what should've been a solid base hit—Butler had one of Kansas City's 13 stolen bases during the AL playoffs. His theft caused a Kansas City area church to change its sign to read: "Thou shalt not steal, unless you are Billy Butler." Photos of the sign went viral.

It was just a small part of the Royals taking a magical ride through the American League playoffs and winning the pennant for the first time since 1985.

"The whole season's been a roller-coaster; we've had a lot of ups and downs but mainly ups lately," Butler said after the AL pennant-clinching game. "We're all brothers in this and we all care about each other. We're 25 playing as one." ■

Above: Billy Butler is the Royals' longest-tenured player. He has been with the club for his entire career, dating back to 2007. Opposite: Butler celebrated his first AL pennant when Kansas City defeated the Baltimore Orioles in the ALCS. (AP Images)

18

OF

RAUL IBANEZ

In Second Stint with K.C., Veteran's Speech Sparks Team

Raul Ibanez had been a productive player for the Royals, batting .286 with 418 hits, 57 home runs, and 252 RBIs during four seasons. But that was 11 years and five teams ago—if you count two stints with Seattle. When the Los Angeles Angels released him on June 21, 2014, he was batting .157 with three homers and 21 RBIs in 57 games, a drastic drop from his 29-homer season last year with Seattle.

Nine days after it appeared Ibanez's 19-year career was finished, why would the Royals sign him?

"We've always been a big admirer of Raul, how he played and how he is as a person," said general manager Dayton Moore, who was more than two seasons away from becoming the Royals general manager when Ibanez left and signed with Seattle after the 2003 season. "We felt by signing him...it makes our team as good as it can be today."

Having hit a ninth-inning game-tying and then a game-winning home run in the 12th inning for the Yankees in Game 3 of the 2012 ALDS, Ibanez had postseason pedigree, making him a more appealing commodity than his meager stats suggested. "I knew that there would be opportunities, and there were multiple opportunities," Ibanez said. "I wanted to get an opportunity to win and be a part of something special. The Royals opportunity was by far the most intriguing one, considering the fact that they gave me the opportunity to play every day. They were the first team that believed in me and gave me a shot."

On the field, the 42-year-old wasn't a great contributor in his second tour with the Royals. After signing on June 30, Ibanez played in 33 games and hit .188 with two home runs and five RBIs. But about three weeks after he signed, he demonstrated why the Royals acquired him.

After taking first place in June, the Royals hit a couple short losing streaks while the Detroit Tigers remained hot. After 98 games Kansas City had lost four in a row and was 48–50, eight games back in the division on July 21. The Royals had been 45–40 on July 4. So after seeing the team slide into a 3–10 funk, Ibanez called a players-only meeting the next afternoon in Chicago.

"I gave them my honest observations and told them about the potential and talent they had," Ibanez said. "I told them that looking in from the outside, every team hated to play them. Everyone saw the talent they had. This was their opportunity."

For the '14 Royals, the speech must've been a turning point. They seized that opportunity. After the speech the Royals defeated the White Sox 7–1. That started a

In his second stint with the Royals, Raul Ibanez warms up prior to a game against the Arizona Diamondbacks on August 6. (AP Images)

five-game winning streak. Whether it had anything to do with the speech or not, throughout the rest of the regular season the Royals went 41–23.

"It's no coincidence. It all started with Raul," Royals left fielder Alex Gordon told *USA TODAY*. "We were kind of in the dumps. We had just been swept coming out of the All-Star break. Things weren't looking good. We came out of that meeting feeling so much different about yourselves."

After the season he had, including not being on the Royals postseason roster after the wild-card, Ibanez is likely to retire and return to his home in the Seattle area with his wife and their family.

"I'm totally fine. I've been blessed," Ibanez told the *New York Post* during the ALCS. "Just being here, being a part of something greater than yourself, is always what it's really about, anyway. It's always about winning. And to get an opportunity to be connected to this team and to Kansas City for the rest of your life, the city will be connected to this team forever. So just to be part of that is phenomenal." ■

Below: Veteran Raul Ibanez speaks during the American League Championship Series. Opposite: About one month after his fiery speech sparked the Royals, Ibanez faces the Texas Rangers on August 24. (AP Images)

8

3B

MIKE MOUSTAKAS

After Demotion to Minors, "Moose" Shines on the Big Stage

All can be forgotten in October...or at least forgiven. That's certainly been the case for Royals third baseman Mike Moustakas, who in 2014 went from a light-hitting punk that spent part of this season in the minors to one of the main reasons the Royals advanced to the World Series for the first time in 29 years.

Starting with the American League playoffs, Moustakas started looking like the player the Royals thought he'd become when they selected him second overall in the 2007 MLB Amateur Draft out of Chatsworth High School in southern California. Taking him behind pitcher David Price seemed like a good gamble. After all, the club wanted an infielder with some pop in his bat. Moustakas, who set the California high school state record with 54 career home runs, hit 24 homers as a high school senior to go with his .577 batting average, and selection as the National Player of the Year by several publications.

Until the 2014 AL playoffs, however, fans hadn't seen that side of Moustakas. He resembled first-round busts of previous years. Saying that "Moose" got off to a slow start in 2014 would be like saying Billy Butler is a slow run-

ner or Greg Holland is an okay closer. Moustakas couldn't have gotten off to a worse start to the season if he tried. The start was so slow that by the time he did pick things up a bit, he couldn't dig out enough to look respectable.

Moustakas didn't exactly help his image off the field during the early part of the season, either. On May 14, "Moose" went 2-for-3 against Colorado in a Kansas City win. The two hits bumped his batting average up to .161, which is still about 40 points below the Mendoza Line, a term, ironically, credited to George Brett during an interview in 1980. Moustakas didn't have any witty comments for reporters. Instead, when asked about his game, he kept responding with comments such as: "[Jason] Vargas threw the ball fantastic," and "Vargie had a great game."

Coincidentally, eight days later, the Royals sent Moustakas and his .152 batting average to Triple A Omaha. At the time it looked as if the club's first-round pick in 2007 (second overall) might be gone for awhile.

"It's the best thing for everybody right now," said general manager Dayton Moore. "You make decisions on what's best for the team and what's best for the player as well. We felt that keeping Moose up as long as we

After defeating the San Francisco Giants in Game 3, Mike Moustakas celebrates with Eric Hosmer. The former prized prospects were selected in the first round in successive drafts. (AP Images)

did gave us the best opportunity to win games at the time. But he understands that it's probably the best for him and the team right now. He's going to go to Omaha and play with that passion and that great heart that he has and get back here and help us, hopefully sooner than later."

Manager Ned Yost, whose players love him because of the confidence he shows in his guys, gave Moustakas a vote of confidence that proved prophetic during the postseason.

"He's a guy that's going to help us win a championship," Yost said in May, when the Royals announced Moustakas' demotion.

The trip to Omaha paid off for both the Storm Chasers and Moustakas. In eight games at Omaha, Moustakas batted .355 with 11 hits. It had taken him nearly a month to get his 11th big league hit this season.

He worked on some mechanics during that stretch, but it didn't seem to make a huge difference once he was back in Kansas City. Moustakas didn't get his batting average to .200 until July 25, but it dipped back down immediately. It didn't surpass .200 "for good" until August 19, the 125th game of the season. He finished with a career-low .212 with 97 hits and 74 strikeouts. He was a mess in the field, too, sporting a career-low .947 fielding percentage at third base.

For some unknown reason, "Moose" broke loose during the American League playoffs, batting .241 with four home runs. He hit 15 home runs during the regular season but only two since July 25 and none in September. (His four homers in the postseason tied him with Willie Aikens for second most postseason home runs in Royals history.) One of Moose's four happened to be the game-winner in the 11th inning at Anaheim.

His defense picked up during the postseason, too. Besides overall solid defensive play, Moustakas robbed Baltimore's Adam Jones of another swing in Game 3 of the ALCS when he went diving into the dugout suite on a play that will forever live in postseason lore. At the time of the play in the sixth inning, the score was tied 1–1, and the Kauffman Stadium crowd had been lulled into the quiet pace of the game. After Moustakas' catch, the stadium became electric again with chants of "Let's go Royals!" mixed in with "Moooooose!"

Whether Moustakas just happened to shine in October or it was his coming-out party, doesn't matter. For now, all else is forgotten. ∎

Above: A Royals fan embraces Mike Moustakas' nickname of "Moose." Opposite: Mike Moustakas hits a solo home run off Bud Norris during Game 2 of the American League Championship Series. (AP Images)

33
P

JAMES SHIELDS

Young Royals Squad Relies on "Big Game James"

The news in December 2012 shocked every baseball insider and fan. The Royals acquired James Shields, an All-Star front-end starting pitcher; Wade Davis, a solid pitcher; and reserve infielder Elliot Johnson (the "player to be named later") from Tampa Bay in a monstrous deal that sent Wil Myers, Jake Odorizzi, Mike Montgomery, and Patrick Leonard to the Rays.

Most "experts" felt general manager Dayton Moore had been bamboozled. Or simply lost his mind. How else could it be explained that he traded Myers, the Baseball America 2012 Player of the Year, for Shields, who's signed through only 2014?

"To be clear: I'm with what seems to be the industry consensus, that the Royals are reaching too far and too early and giving up too much," Sam Mellinger, columnist for the *Kansas City Star*.

Former *Star* columnist and *Sports Illustrated* writer Joe Posnanski was a little bolder in his assessment of the trade: "I despise the Royals' trade of late Sunday night. Despise. Deplore. Deride. Disapprove."

One of the few who lauded the deal was Fox Sports writer Ken Rosenthal, who wrote: "This is a chance that the Royals had to take, not just for Moore to save his job, but also for the franchise to restore its good name... now, they should at least compete in the AL Central, even with the mighty Tigers."

And that's exactly what the Royals did with Shields. He was a big reason in 2013 the Royals were in the hunt for their first postseason berth since 1985 and their first winning record since 2003. (They were eliminated from the wild-card during the final week of the regular season and finished third in the AL Central with an 86–76 record, their best since 1989.) "Big Game James" Shields went 13–9 with a 3.15 ERA in 34 starts. Additionally, he struck out 196 while walking only 68. In September Shields had a 4–1 record with a 3.18 ERA and 44 strikeouts in six starts. His strikeout total was the most for the Royals in September since Bret Saberhagen fanned 48 in 1989.

Shields had nearly identical numbers in 2014, as he went 14–8 with a 3.21 ERA in 34 starts. He was in or near the top 10 in most categories for starting pitchers in the American League.

"He knows how to handle his emotions and channel it to his benefit, but he also knows how to transfer it to his teammates," Royals manager Ned Yost said. "He knows what's at stake and he's getting after it. He's into it."

James Shields, who went 14–8 with a 3.21 ERA during the 2014 season, throws during a July 12th contest against the Detroit Tigers. (AP Images)

Shields was into it so much that he made three starts during the American League playoffs, including the wild-card game against Oakland and the first game of the ALCS against Baltimore.

In those three games, Shields was roughed up, but he went 16 total innings and came away with a 1–0 record. (Had the Orioles defeated Kansas City in Game 4, Shields was slated to start Game 5 in Kansas City.) With plenty of rest, Shields was the Royals' Game 1 starter in the World Series. Again, he was roughed up, but by starting him, it proved the confidence Yost has in his ace.

"He's very competitive and he's a guy that when his stuff is right he's dominant," Yost said. "But you have to know James Shields. You have to know that he's a tremendous competitor. He has the ability to make adjustments. Right now he just hasn't been as sharp as he has been."

As important as what Shields can do on the mound is what he's done in the clubhouse. He quickly became a veteran leader for the young pitchers and he brought a fun but winning attitude. After every win this season, including during the postseason, the players had a mini-celebration, complete with a fog machine, strobe lights, and the introduction of a Player of the Game. Shields was behind that.

"If we used to win in a game, we'd come in the clubhouse, and you really couldn't tell," pitching mate Danny Duffy told mlb.com during the ALCS. "Now we've got music jumping. Every win has meaning. Everything, really, has meaning. Even losses, they hurt more. Everything we do matters. Every pitch. Every at-bat. It's big.

"One of the most genius moves anyone's ever made in baseball was to get him...It changed our clubhouse. It changed our organization. It's night and day from what it was when I first got here." ■

James Shields showed his mettle during the ALCS—he pitched with a kidney stone during Game 1 and was in "excruciating pain." (AP Images)

A Long Time Coming

Victory Against White Sox Clinches First Playoff Berth Since '85

Twenty-nine years is a lifetime for some. But there they were, the newest crop of Royals—half of whom weren't alive in October 1985—on September 26, the final Friday of the regular season, still trailing the Tigers by one game but with a chance to clinch at least one of the two wild-card spots.

With two outs in the bottom of the ninth and the Royals leading the White Sox 3–1 and hundreds of Royals fans in the U.S. Cellular Field stands chanting "Let's go Royals," closer Greg Holland got Michael Taylor to pop up in foul territory. Catcher Salvador Perez threw his mask aside and camped under the ball. As soon as he secured it, the years of waiting, anticipation, and even embarrassment were coming to a close.

The Royals were going to the postseason.

It sparked a celebration in the clubhouse and on the field with the fans that would've given the '85 World Series celebration a run for its money.

"I live within my own heart," an emotional Royals manager Ned Yost said. "I know what these guys can do. I don't need somebody to tell me what they can do or what they can't do. I've been telling you guys for two or three years that this is a club that has the opportunity to go the playoffs and win a world championship. I believed it."

With a large contingency of Royals fans from Kansas City, Chicago, and all points in between at the game, the offense took a load off pitcher Jeremy Guthrie's shoulders in the first inning. After Alcides Escobar led off the first with a single, Nori Aoki tripled to right, giving Kansas City a 1–0 lead. Lorenzo Cain then knocked in Aoki with a base hit to center. Cain stole second base before coming in to score on a single by Billy Butler.

That was more than Guthrie needed. He gave up only four hits and held the White Sox scoreless during seven innings of work. Yost then turned to two-thirds of the club's three-headed bullpen monster. Wade Davis surrendered Chicago's only run of the contest, but Greg Holland retired the Sox in order in the ninth as he picked up his 46th save of the season.

"If we could get a couple of runs for Guthrie early and give him some breathing room," Yost said. "I had a feeling he was going to be really sharp today and he was."

After the team celebrated in the clubhouse for a while, they came back out onto the field and started high-fiving and celebrating with their fans.

With two games left and trailing Detroit by only one, the Royals had a prime opportunity to force a one-game playoff with the Tigers to determine the division champ.

Something, though, that would become more rewarding happened. Both teams lost on Saturday and both won on Sunday. So the Royals, instead of playing the Baltimore Orioles in the ALDS, would be playing host to the Oakland A's in the wild-card game. Although that sounds like a more difficult road, that contest sparked one of the greatest, most magical stretches in Kansas City baseball history. ■

Eric Hosmer celebrates with catcher Salvador Perez following the Royals' 3–1 win over the Chicago White Sox on September 26. The win clinched a postseason berth for the Royals. (AP Images)

Clad in playoff t-shirts, Royals fans at Kauffman Stadium celebrate during the playoffs. (AP Images)

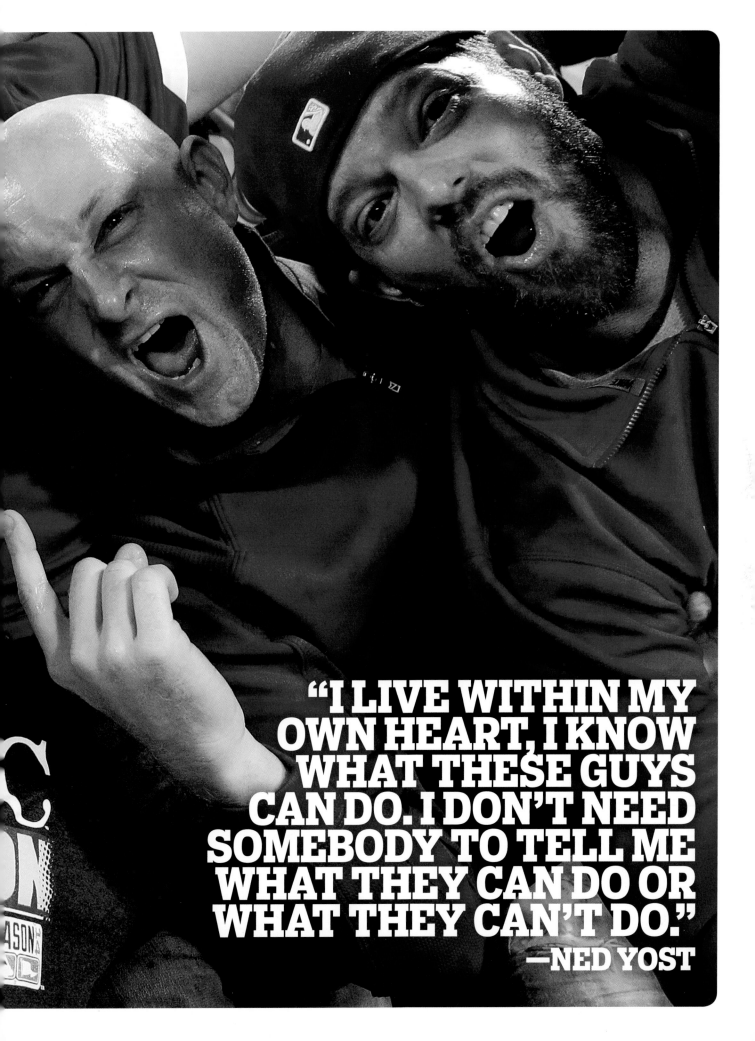

"I LIVE WITHIN MY OWN HEART. I KNOW WHAT THESE GUYS CAN DO. I DON'T NEED SOMEBODY TO TELL ME WHAT THEY CAN DO OR WHAT THEY CAN'T DO."
—NED YOST

American League PLAYOFFS

Billy Butler, the Royals' longest tenured player, is introduced before the wild card game against the A's. (AP Images)

Putting the Wild in Wild Card
Royals Swipe Seven Bases to Spur Epic Comeback

Well, that was fast. Or so it initially seemed. Twenty-nine years of waiting, of frustration, of thinking every spring "maybe this is our year," to the midsummer realization "there's always next year." After 29 years the Royals were finally here, in the postseason. And in less than 29 minutes—or however long it took Oakland to put together a five-run sixth inning—it was over. This time of the year teams don't come back from 7–3 deficits after seven innings, especially a team like Kansas City that had spent so much energy during the roller-coaster 2014 season just to reach the postseason.

But in front of a rocking, standing-room only crowd of 40,502 at Kauffman Stadium, the young and inexperienced Royals were brought back to life in the wildest of wild card games. And all it took were two pinch-hitters, seven stolen bases, seven pitchers, a batter who had been 0-for-5, and 12 innings.

"This will go down as the craziest game I've ever played," first baseman Eric Hosmer said. "This team showed a lot of character. No one believed in us before the game. No one believed in us before the season."

Pitcher Jon Lester, whom Oakland acquired at the trade deadline for an anticipated postseason run, held a comfortable 7–3 lead. That was bad news for the Royals considering Lester has had Kansas City's number throughout his career, regardless of the name on his uniform. In fact, Lester, who was 4–0 against the Royals in 2014, shut out Kansas City in Boston on July 20, and then two starts later, on August 2—his first appearance for the A's—he beat the Royals again.

But things would change after the seventh inning of the wild-card game.

Down to six outs and nothing to lose against Lester, the Royals tightened the screws a little. Alcides Escobar led off the bottom of the eighth with a base hit and then promptly stole a base, one of seven on the night for the Royals. After Nori Aoki advanced Escobar with a ground-out to second, Lorenzo Cain singled to center. That made it 7–4 Oakland. With Hosmer at the plate, Cain stole second. Hosmer walked, which ended Lester's night. Relief pitcher Luke Gregerson gave up a single to Billy Butler, scoring Cain and moving Hosmer to third. 7–5 Oakland. Terrance Gore, running for Butler, stole second. Perhaps focusing too much on Kansas City's speed on the basepath, Gregerson threw a wild pitch to Alex Gordon that

Royals' 12th-inning hero Eric Hosmer scores a single by Christian Colon, tying the game at 8–8. (AP Images)

scored Hosmer on a dive at home. 7–6 Oakland. Gordon ended up walking and then stole second. (In case you're not keeping track, that's four stolen bases for the Royals in the inning.) The inning came to a screeching halt, though, as Gregerson struck out both Salvador Perez and Omar Infante. It was the second time in the game that the hitless Perez struck out. He'd get another chance.

The Royals tied the game in the bottom of the ninth, courtesy of pinch-hitter Josh Willingham, who was a late-season acquisition brought in to give Kansas City some veteran power at the plate. Hitting for Mike Moustakas against Oakland reliever Sean Doolittle, Willingham blooped a base hit. Jarrod Dyson, running for Willingham, was sacrificed to second and then stole third. He tied the game on a sacrifice fly by Aoki.

After Brandon Finnegan, who barely three months earlier was pitching for Texas Christian University in the College World Series, relieved Greg Holland and shut down the A's, the Royals seemed to be on their way to the American League Division Series. Hosmer led off the Kansas City 10th with an infield base hit and advanced to second on a sacrifice by pinch-hitter Christian Colon. Two batters later, with Hosmer at third and two outs, Perez had a chance to redeem his eighth-inning strikeout. But the Royals All-Star catcher grounded out to second, making him hitless in five at-bats.

After neither team scored in the 11th, former Royal Alberto Callaspo delivered a pinch-hit RBI single off Finnegan that scored Josh Reddick and gave the A's an 8–7 lead.

"First postseason in 29 years?" Finnegan said after the game. "I felt like I just ended it."

Yet, once again, just when it looked as if the Royals might be finished for the season, they gave everyone a foreshadowing to the next two weeks.

Eric Hosmer slides in to a score on a wild pitch by relief pitcher Luke Gregerson in the eighth inning, reducing the A's lead to 7–6. (AP Images)

With one out in the 12th, Hosmer tripled off the top of the wall in left-center. Colon, another rookie, knocked in Hosmer and reached safely on a high chopper to third base. That tied the ballgame. Colon then stole second—the seventh swipe of the night for Kansas City—giving the Royals a runner in scoring position with two outs and Perez at the plate once again.

"I worry about it because I want to help the team," Perez said.

Perez, who looked silly throughout the game at the plate, reached out for a low and away pitch with two strikes and pulled the ball past diving third baseman Josh Donaldson. Colon, who has good speed, scored easily, giving the Royals a walk-off win—their first post-season victory since Game 7 of the 1985 World Series.

"That's the most incredible game I've ever been a part of," Royals manager Ned Yost said. "Our guys never quit. We fell behind there in the fifth inning, sixth inning. They kept battling back. They weren't going to be denied. It was just a great game."

Of course, it was a controversial decision Yost made in the sixth inning that helped lead to Oakland's runs. Starter James Shields gave up a bloop single to Sam Fuld and then walked Donaldson. With two on and nobody out and Kansas City holding a 3–2 lead with Brandon Moss—who homered earlier—coming to the plate, Yost pulled Shields, who'd thrown 88 pitches, and brought in starter Yordano Ventura. Yosted! Instead of going to a reliever, Yost pulled "Big Game James" and brought in another starter, a questionable move by the much-maligned manager. Moss sent Ventura's third pitch 432 feet to dead center.

"Just one of those things," Yost said.

But despite those things, this was just the beginning of something special for the Royals.

"It was absolutely epic," Shields said. "You don't write a story like that." ■

Outfielder Lorenzo Cain (center) celebrates the Royals' victory over the A's. Cain drove in two runs in the wild-card game. (AP Images)

Hometown Moose Breaks Loose

Ex-Angel Vargas, Great D Stymie L.A. in Extra Innings

With Kansas City's dramatic win over Oakland in the wild-card game, the Royals earned the right to play the best team in baseball, the Los Angeles Angels of Anaheim, in a best-of-five series, with the first two games in Anaheim. That didn't seem to phase the Royals.

Two nights after beating the A's in 12 innings, the Royals used extra frames again, this time to beat the Angels 3–2 in 11 innings.

In the top of the 11th inning—with the scored tied 2–2—the No. 9 hitter, Mike Moustakas, a Los Angeles native, belted a 374-foot home run to right field that reached the elevated seats off reliever Fernando Salas and gave Kansas City a 3–2 lead.

"It's probably the biggest one I've ever hit," Moustakas said. "It felt really amazing."

That was the Royals first hit since the fifth inning, when they took a 2–1 lead against starter Jered Weaver. Alex Gordon led off the fifth with a double, moved to third on a Salvador Perez fly out, and then scored on a sacrifice fly by Omar Infante.

The Angels tied the game in the bottom of the fifth when David Freese led off with a homer to left field off Kansas City's surprise starter Jason Vargas, who was 1–5 in his last six starts and hadn't won since September 3.

Against his former Angels mates, Vargas looked more like the pitcher who had ended April with a 2.40 ERA. He gave up three hits and two runs—both on solo home runs—in six innings.

Kansas City's defense helped Vargas' line look better than it could have. Center fielder Lorenzo Cain made two spectacular grabs, including one at the wall in the first inning struck by Anaheim's leadoff hitter, Kole Calhoun. Right fielder Nori Aoki got in on the action as well with two outstanding catches, including a run-saving snag against the wall in the sixth. On the play Cain and Aoki both gave chase, but after Cain missed it high on the wall, Aoki was there to record the out.

"This game was won by Kansas City with four incredible defensive plays," Angels manager Mike Scioscia said. "That's what really kept those guys in the game."

Danny Duffy, whom many thought would get the start, pitched the 10th inning and got the win. After Moustakas' homer in the 11th inning, Greg Holland, who arrived at the stadium in the fourth inning following a trip to North Carolina for the birth of his son, shut the door on the Angels with a perfect 11th.

"This is the type of game that we play," Royals manager Ned Yost said. "We don't score a bunch of runs...so we have a lot of confidence in our pitching." ■

Mike Moustakas, who hit only 15 homers during the regular season, celebrates his 11th inning home run in Game 1. The blast proved to be the game winner. (AP Images)

Mike Moustakas connects on his home run off the Angels' Fernando Salas in the 11th inning of Game 1. (AP Images)

"IT'S PROBABLY THE BIGGEST ONE I'VE EVER HIT, IT FELT REALLY AMAZING."

—MIKE MOUSTAKAS

"THIS GAME WAS WON BY KANSAS CITY WITH FOUR INCREDIBLE DEFENSIVE PLAYS, THAT'S WHAT REALLY KEPT THOSE GUYS IN THE GAME."
—ANGELS MANAGER MIKE SCIOSCIA

Center fielder Lorenzo Cain and right fielder Nori Aoki race toward the right-center field wall. Aoki's running catch of a deep fly ball off the bat of Howie Kendrick prevented a run from scoring and ended the inning. (AP Images)

Homer for Hosmer

Underdog Royals Eek Out 2–0 Series Lead Against Mighty Angels

For a third consecutive game, the Royals went into extra innings. For the third consecutive game, they won. For a third consecutive game, it was a homegrown player who came through in the clutch.

With Game 2 of the ALDS tied at 1–1 in the top of the 11th inning after Lorenzo Cain beat out an infield single, Eric Hosmer launched a 399-foot homer to right with a picture-perfect swing at Angel Stadium of Anaheim. It was Hosmer's third hit of the game. Later in the inning, Alex Gordon, who knocked in Kansas City's first run back in the second inning, scored on a base hit by Salvador Perez giving the Royals their eventual 4–1 win.

"Everyone has had their time," Hosmer said. "They've had their moment when they've made a big play or stepped up and did something big. A lot of the times, it was with our back against the wall. Most of the time it was with our season on the line."

The script of that streak, which Hollywood would turn down as too unbelievable, started in the wild-card game when Perez, who signed as an undrafted free agent in 2006, nearly four months after Dayton Moore became general manager, knocked in Christian Colon in the 12th inning in Kansas City. It continued in Game 1 of the ALDS, when Mike Moustakas, the Royals' first-round pick (second overall) in 2007, launched a home run in the 11th. The blast by Hosmer, Kansas City's first-round pick (third overall) in 2008, gave the Royals a 2–0 lead in the series.

Besides the Royals—baseball's lowest home run producer during the regular season—winning with another long ball, the club had another outfield play that helped preserve the game. In the bottom of the eighth with no outs and pinch-runner Collin Cowgill at second, Jarrod Dyson caught Chris Iannetta's fly ball in left-center. Cowgill tested Dyson's arm. Bad move. Dyson threw a strike to Moustakas, completing the double play.

"That's huge," Hosmer said. "That changes momentum. That changes everything in a game right there."

Rookie Brandon Finnegan, whom the Royals selected in the first round (17th overall) in the June 2014 draft and who had an outstanding performance in the wild-card game, pitched a hitless 10th and won his first game of the postseason. For the second consecutive night, Greg Holland saved it for the Royals.

A night after the crafty Jason Vargas kept the Angels in check, the flame-throwing Yordano Ventura started for Kansas City and scattered five hits over seven innings. He struck out five and walked only one.

"His stuff was electric," Angels third baseman David Freese said of Ventura, who eclipsed 100 miles per hour on the radar gun numerous times. "They've got good arms over there, and they're making the plays, getting timely hits, and doing what they need to do to win." ▪

Eric Hosmer connects on a two-run homer in the 11th inning of Game 2. (AP Images)

"EVERYONE HAS HAD THEIR TIME.... A LOT OF THE TIME, IT WAS WITH OUR BACK AGAINST THE WALL. MOST OF THE TIME IT WAS WITH OUR SEASON ON THE LINE."
—ERIC HOSMER

After his first of three hits in Game 2, Eric Hosmer scores on a single by Alex Gordon. (AP Images)

Rookie Yordano Ventura started for the Royals and allowed only one run in seven innings. (AP Images)

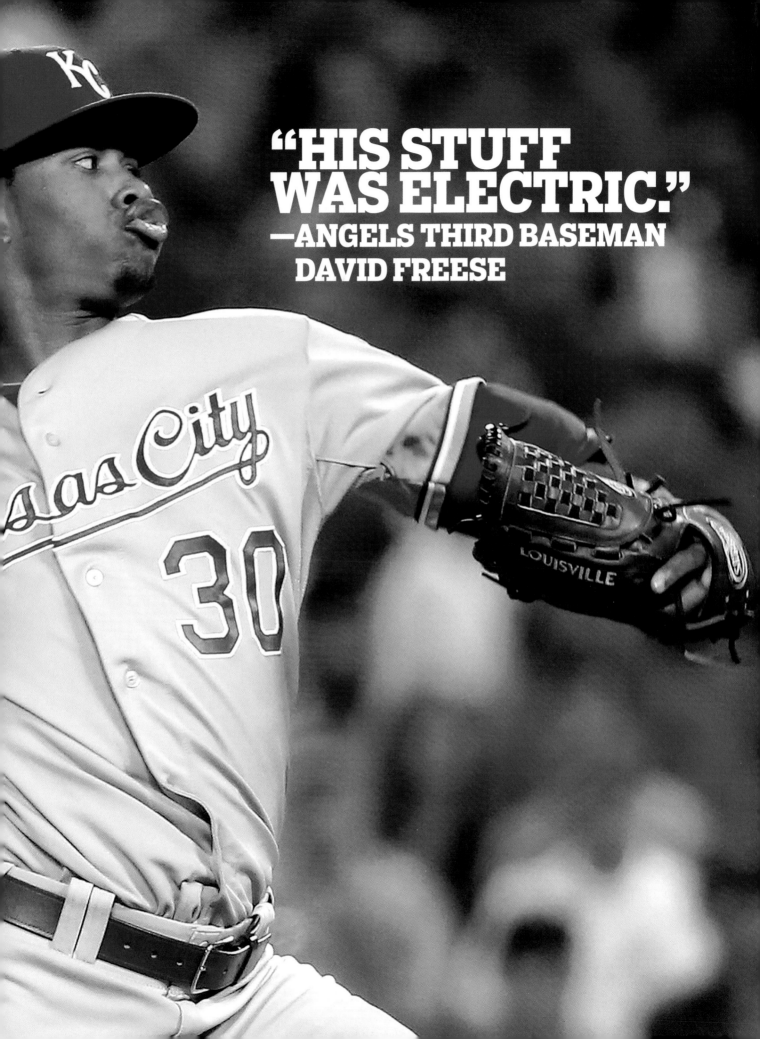

"HIS STUFF WAS ELECTRIC."
—ANGELS THIRD BASEMAN DAVID FREESE

A Royal Sweep

No Extra Innings Needed as K.C. Roughs Up L.A.

In front of another rambunctious standing-room crowd (40,657) at Kauffman Stadium, the Royals rested the extra-inning drama for a game as they jumped on Angels starter C.J. Wilson early en route to an 8–3 win and a three-game sweep of the Angels in the American League Division Series.

Trailing 1–0 after a Mike Trout home run—the first hit of the series for the superstar—the Royals got three runs in the bottom of the first thanks to a bases-loaded double by Alex Gordon that scored Nori Aoki, Lorenzo Cain, and Billy Butler and gave Kansas City a 3–1 lead. That hit also knocked Wilson out of the game after just two-thirds of an inning.

"Trout hit that home run, and it was good for us to respond like we did," Gordon said. "Good job by the guys getting on base and making something happen and putting me in a good situation."

The Royals put the game out of reach in the third when Eric Hosmer hit his second home run of the ALDS—a 427-foot bomb to center—that put the Royals ahead 5–1.

"Big Game James" Shields gave up two solo home runs but otherwise battled, pitching the type of game Royals fans expected out of him in a possible series-ending contest. Shields, who was making his first start since the wild-card game, scattered six hits over six innings. As was the case for Royals pitchers throughout the previous three postseason games, Shields was aided by his defense. Specifically, back-to-back diving catches in center by Cain in the fifth inning with two on and one out.

"You're probably looking at a one- or two-run game if both those hits drop in, but they didn't," Angels manager Mike Scioscia said.

Things seemed to be going Kansas City's way the entire game. Case in point: in the bottom of the third, after Hosmer's home run, Butler walked. And, get this, Billy Butler, the man who usually runs as if he's carrying a piano and the only lumbering hitter in a lineup full of speedsters, stole second. It was his fifth career steal and his first since July 5, 2012.

After Shields went six innings for the victory, the usual relief Herrera-Davis-Holland troika finished off the Angels, combining for seven strikeouts.

They—like the rest of their teammates—looked quite comfortable taking down the team with the best record in the American League.

"I've never seen this group of kids so confident on the big stage," Royals manager Ned Yost said. "It's really fun to see their development and watch them come into the postseason and just really take their game to the next level."

And, after making quick work of the Angels, the Royals were headed to the next level of the playoffs. For the first time since 1985, Kansas City was going to be playing for a trip to the World Series.

"This is a special time in this city right now," Shields said, "and they're enjoying this as much as we are." ■

Starting pitcher James Shields reacts after striking out Chris Iannetta to end the sixth inning. Shields pitched six innings in the series clincher and gave up just two runs, both on solo homers. (AP Images)

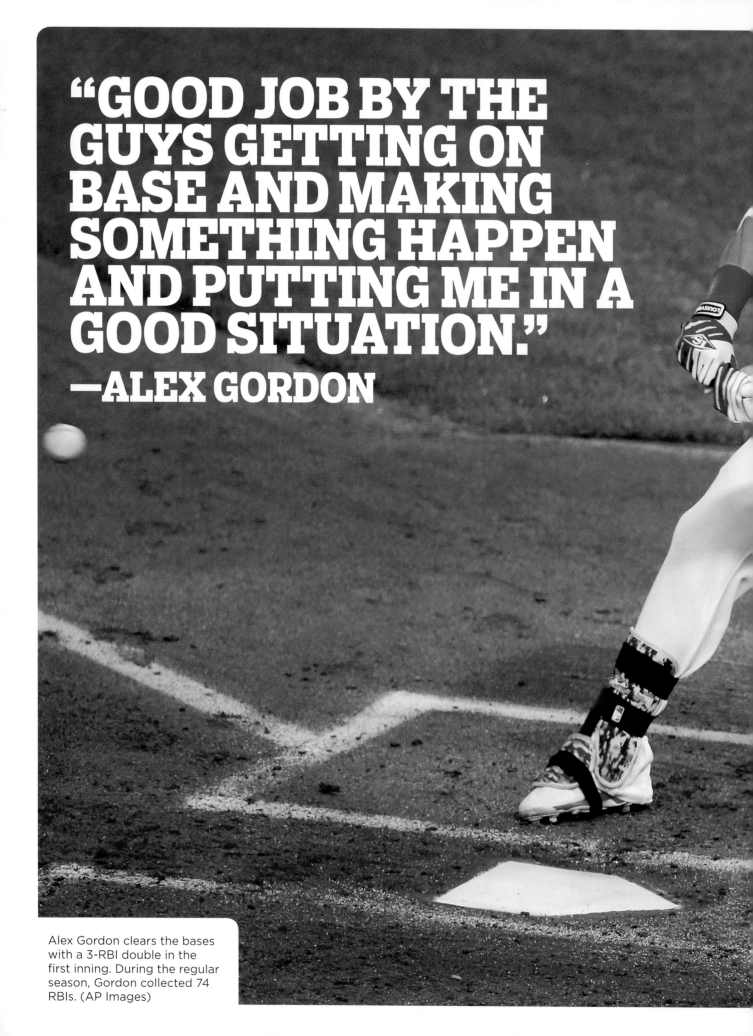

"GOOD JOB BY THE GUYS GETTING ON BASE AND MAKING SOMETHING HAPPEN AND PUTTING ME IN A GOOD SITUATION."
—ALEX GORDON

Alex Gordon clears the bases with a 3-RBI double in the first inning. During the regular season, Gordon collected 74 RBIs. (AP Images)

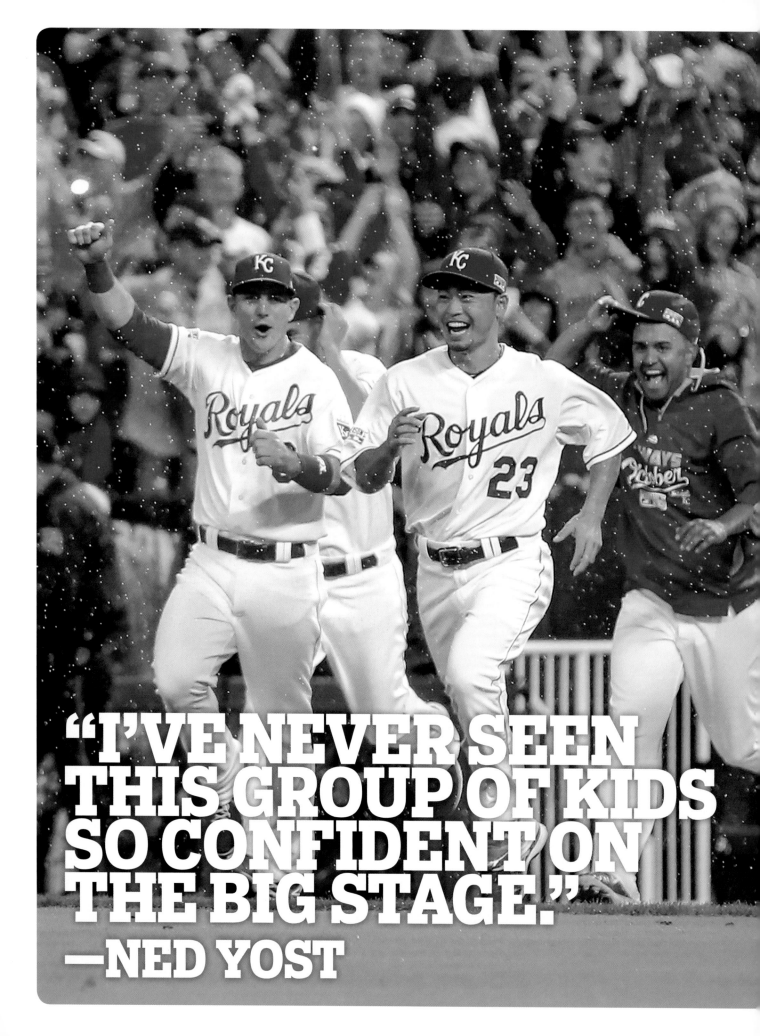

"I'VE NEVER SEEN THIS GROUP OF KIDS SO CONFIDENT ON THE BIG STAGE."
—NED YOST

Royals players erupt from the dugout to celebrate their ALDS sweep of the Angels. (AP Images)

The Royals' division series celebration moved from the field to the clubhouse, as Kansas City celebrated its first win in a postseason series in 29 years. The celebration continued past midnight. Eric Hosmer extended an invitation for fans to meet the team at Kansas City's McFadden's bar, where players reportedly picked up a $15,000 bar tab. (AP Images)

Power Surge

Gordon, Butler Homer in 10th as Royals Win Another Extra-Inning Affair

Ask Mike Moustakas—the author of an extra-inning home run in Game 1 of the American League Division Series—if he's one of the leaders of this team and he'll deflect the question and point to Alex Gordon.

"He's our backbone," Moustakas said. "He's our heart and soul. He's our leader."

Gordon, the Royals' Gold Glove left fielder, carried the Royals on his back in Game 1 of the American League Championship Series in Baltimore.

In yet another extra-inning affair—the fourth in five games for the Royals—Gordon had a dramatic George Brett-esque night for Kansas City. An at-bat after being plunked in the neck by Andrew Miller, Gordon launched a lead-off home run off Darren O'Day into the dark Baltimore sky in the 10th inning that put the Royals ahead 6–5. For good measure, three batters later, Moustakas added a two-run homer. It's a good thing. The Orioles scored a run in the bottom of the inning, making the final 8–6 in favor of the Royals.

"Just trying to put a good at-bat together, get on base any way I could," Gordon said after the game when asked about his approach against O'Day. "And sometimes you just get a good pitch to hit and you put a good swing on it and those things happen. So usually when you're not trying to hit a home run is when you do it. I was just trying to get a base hit."

"[Gordon is] a guy that can get hit by a pitch and do exactly what he did, drive it out of the ballpark tonight, after getting hit in the neck," said Royals manager Ned Yost. "So it was a huge hit for us at that point because we were really trying hard to get Greg Holland in that game and that allowed it."

After using the three-headed monster of Kelvin Herrera, Wade Davis, and Holland out of the bullpen against Oakland in the wild card game trying to hold the A's, Yost has been using his relievers to give Holland a chance to pitch in extra innings. That worked out perfectly in Game 1 of the ALCS. Herrera and Davis each went two innings, which set up Holland for a stressful 10th. Holland recorded two quick outs, but after giving up a hit and a walk, Delmon Young knocked in Ryan Flaherty with a base hit, and cut Kansas City's lead to two runs. Holland then got Orioles leadoff batter Nick Markakis to ground out and end the game.

But pitching has not been a problem spot for the

Alex Gordon breaks the tie in the top of the 10th inning with his solo home run. (AP Images)

Royals this season. The most glaring dent in the armor of this team has been power. The Angels and now Orioles might disagree. Besides homers by Gordon and Moustakas, Alcides Escobar led off the third inning with his fourth home run of 2014. Three home runs in the game and now seven in five postseason games. Not bad for a club that had the fewest in the majors (95) compared to Baltimore's major league-leading 211.

"[Baltimore is] a great team, a homer team, and for us, everybody is talking about speed. But everybody can hit the ball, like Gordon and Moose," Escobar said. "For me, I was just trying to put the ball in play."

And, as has been the case during the postseason, good things have happened for the Royals when they've just "put the ball in play."

Later in the third, with Kansas City leading 1–0 after Escobar's home run, Gordon helped give Kansas City

Above: Mike Moustakas drove in four runs, including his two-run homer in the 10th inning. The two Game 1 home runs brought the Royals' total to seven in their first five postseason games. Opposite: Starter James Shields, who posted a 3.21 ERA during the regular season, throws during the first inning. (AP Images)

what seemed to be a safe lead. With the bases loaded, Gordon dropped a three-run, broken bat double down the right-field line against starter Chris Tillman. Nori Aoki, Lorenzo Cain, and Billy Butler scored, putting the Royals on top, 4–0.

Baltimore got on the board in the bottom of the third before Gordon made a spectacular defensive play. Markakis led off the inning with a double to right. Alejandro De Aza advanced him to third on a ground-out to Omar Infante. Adam Jones then knocked in Markakis with a hit to left against Kansas City starter James Shields. After Nelson Cruz fouled out to Salvador Perez, Gordon saved a run by turning on the speed at the last minute and making a sliding catch a few feet from the warning track in the left-field gap on a ball struck by Steve Pearce.

"When I saw [center fielder Cain] kind of looking at me I knew it was my ball," Gordon said. "I think it kind of came back to me a little bit and just tried to make the catch at the last second."

At the plate Gordon went 3-for-4 with four RBIs and a run scored. Adding to his three-run double in the finale of the ALDS against Anaheim, Gordon is the second player in major league history with two three-run doubles in a single postseason. The other was Graig Nettles of the Yankees, who did it in 1981.

Coincidentally, one day shy of exactly 29 years ago—on Friday, October 11, 1985—Brett had one of his most memorable postseason games when he went 4-for-4 with two homers and a double, and he scored four of the club's six runs in a win against Toronto in Game 3. And, as with Gordon's run-saving play in the outfield in the third, Brett made one of the best defensive plays of his career when he backhanded a grounder and threw out Damaso Garcia at home plate. ▪

Lorenzo Cain, Nori Aoki, and Billy Butler celebrate after scoring on a bases-clearing double by Alex Gordon in the third inning to give the Royals an early 4–0 lead. (AP Images)

American League Championship Series: Game 2
October 11, 2014 • Royals 6, Orioles 4

Cain Is Able

Outfielder's 4 Hits Pace Royals to 2-0 Series Lead

Lorenzo Cain's wife Jenny gave birth to the couple's first baby, Cameron Loe, three days before the ALCS began. Four days later, daddy put on a performance that Cameron will one day tell his kids about.

Cain, who was on base four times and scored two runs in Game 1, went 4-for-5 with two runs and an RBI in Kansas City's 6–4 win in Game 2 of the ALCS at Camden Yards. Cain joins George Brett as the only Royals with four hits in a postseason game. (Brett did it twice.) Adding to Cain's day at the plate, he made two more outstanding plays in the outfield.

After four extra-inning contests in the postseason, including Game 1 of this series, the Royals broke a 4–4 tie with two runs in the top of the ninth inning. It started innocently enough when Omar Infante dribbled an infield single off pitcher Darren O'Day. With Terrance Gore running for Infante, Mike Moustakas laid down a sacrifice bunt that moved Gore to second. From there the speedy Gore had no trouble scoring on a double by Alcides Escobar. Two batters later, after Jarrod Dyson reached on an error, Cain got his fourth hit of the game, this one scoring Escobar.

It seems ironic now that along with Cain, Escobar was a major piece of the trade that sent Zack Greinke to Milwaukee in 2010. Now, both of those players key a Royals win in the postseason. (Incidentally, another player coming from the Brewers in that deal was pitcher Jake Odorizzi, who was one of the four players the Royals sent to Tampa in 2012 to get James Shields and Wade Davis.)

"That [Milwaukee trade] was the start of putting together a championship caliber baseball team, to get two guys as athletic as they are and in a trade," said Royals manager Ned Yost.

"[Cain and Escobar] were special to me," he added. "They were very athletic. I brought those kids up to the big leagues to play in Spring Training whenever I had the opportunity and they were at A-ball or Double A at that time. So they were always fun to watch. You could see Escobar was a little more advanced than Lorenzo Cain. Lorenzo was really raw at that time. But you could tell with his athleticism that one day he might turn into one heck of a player, and he sure has."

And Cain, who didn't play organized baseball until his sophomore year of high school, is showing that on one of baseball's biggest stages. As we're getting used to seeing during this postseason, Cain made two spectacular catches—one that was simply incredible and one that might've saved the game for the Royals.

Outfielder Lorenzo Cain, who went 4-for-5 in Game 2, reacts after stealing second base in the fifth inning. (AP Images)

"IF YOU CAN GO HOME 2–0, THAT'S AS GOOD AS IT GETS. GOING HOME 2–0 WITH OUR CROWD FOR THE NEXT THREE DAYS IS GOING TO BE EXCITING."
—NED YOST

In the sixth inning, J.J. Hardy led off with what appeared to be a double (or more) to the gap in right-center. In a flash that would make Superman envious, Cain flew through the air and made a spectacular diving catch. MLB's Statcast calculated that Cain covered 82 feet in 3.65 seconds, reaching a top speed of 21.2 miles per hour.

Then in the bottom of the seventh, after Yost made his usual late-inning base running and defensive move, putting Dyson in center and Cain in right, Cain saved the game for the Royals. With the bases loaded and two outs in a 4–4 game, Hardy lifted a soft fly ball toward the right-field line. As he did an inning earlier, Cain came from out of nowhere and robbed Hardy, this time saving at least two runs.

"I thought for sure that ball was going to drop when it first left the bat," said Yost. "And then all of a sudden here he comes and makes the play. The country is seeing a very exciting player in Lorenzo Cain."

"He makes one in center, then moves to right and makes one there," Orioles manager Buck Showalter said. "I expected him to make one in left field before the game was over."

Billy Butler hits an RBI double in the third, scoring Lorenzo Cain. (AP Images)

Cain helped give Kansas City the lead with his bat in the first inning off Baltimore starting pitcher Bud Norris with a one-out double that moved Nori Aoki to third. The next batter, Eric Hosmer, singled in both Aoki and Cain. After Baltimore scored a run in the second, the Royals got back to a two-run lead in the third, thanks largely to Cain. With two outs and nobody on, Cain reached on an infield single to Hardy. After Hosmer singled, Billy Butler roped an RBI double to right that scored Cain.

Baltimore tied the game at 3–3 with two runs in the bottom of the third only to see Kansas City add a run in the top of the fourth. This time it was courtesy of a two-out solo home run by Moustakas, his fourth homer in six postseason games. That ties Moustakas with Willie Aikens for most home runs by a Royals player in the postseason. Aikens had four against Philadelphia in the 1980 World Series.

Yordano Ventura started the game for Kansas City and cruised through the first inning. That was the only time when he looked smooth. In fact, Ventura left the game with two outs in the sixth because of tightness in his throwing shoulder. Ventura gave up four runs on five hits and three walks in five and two-third innings. Wade Davis eventually got the win, his second in the postseason, and Greg Holland pitched the ninth for his second save in the ALCS.

This marked the first time the Orioles have lost consecutive games at Camden Yards since June 28–29, when they lost two to Tampa Bay.

As they had done a few days earlier, the Royals were headed back to rowdy Kauffman Stadium with a two games to none lead against a heavily favored club.

"If you could go home 1–1, you're going to be really, really happy," manager Ned Yost said. "If you can go home 2–0, that's as good as it gets. Going home 2–0 with our crowd for the next three days is going to be exciting." ■

Mike Moustakas celebrates his solo home run. The blast was Moustakas' fourth round-tripper in six postseason games, tying Willie Mays Aikens' team record. (AP Images)

One Win Away

Defense, Bullpen Key as Royals Take 3-0 Lead

Due to rain, the Royals had to wait an extra day to see if they could continue their undefeated postseason streak. Whether it was the weather or the late-night games leading up to the Tuesday night Game 3 contest against Baltimore, the Kauffman Stadium crowd seemed tame. They certainly were more subdued than in the two earlier postseason games against the A's and Angels.

That all changed in the top of the sixth inning against the Orioles. With the scored tied 1–1 and Jason Frasor relieving starting pitcher Jeremy Guthrie, Baltimore's Adam Jones popped a ball in foul territory beyond third base. Although it looked as if it was headed for the seats, Mike Moustakas tracked it the whole way and, as the wind pushed it back over the dugout, reached out and flipped into the dugout suite as he made the catch.

"I knew the wind was blowing out hard to right, so I was just talking to myself, hoping it would blow back," Moustakas said. "It blew back just enough for me to make the play."

And then it happened. As if snapping out of a daydream, Kauffman Stadium became electric again with chants of "Let's Go Royals!" ringing from the crowd of 40,183.

"It really did fire up the whole stadium," first baseman Eric Hosmer said after the game.

Frasor ended up pitching a perfect sixth. The crowd remained in a frenzy in the bottom half of the inning, with Jarrod Dyson on third, Billy Butler lifted a sacrifice fly to deep left that broke the tie and gave Kansas City a 2–1 lead. That's how the score would stand as the Royals took a three games to none lead.

"We've got a snowball effect going right now," Butler said. "The confidence couldn't be any higher."

Moose's play in the sixth was just one of several defensive gems turned in by the Royals, who finished 21st in the Majors in fielding in 2014 with 104 errors, the most by any of the four remaining teams—Baltimore (87), St. Louis (88), and San Francisco (100).

In fact, Moustakas, who's been an offensive threat during the postseason, had another outstanding key play in the fourth inning when he dove to his left and snagged a hard liner by Steve Pearce. That was a potentially big play because in the second, Pearce scored Baltimore's lone run of the game when he doubled and then was knocked in on a double by the next hitter, J.J. Hardy.

"From where I was standing, I didn't see any way he could get a glove on that ball," said Royals manager Ned

Third baseman Mike Moustakas makes a gravity-defying catch on a ball hit by Baltimore's Adam Jones in the sixth inning. (AP Images)

Yost. "Just tremendous reactions, made a tremendous play on that."

Hosmer made top-rate plays, robbing Nelson Cruz of a hit in the second when he dove and touched the bag just ahead of Cruz, and then on a ball ripped by Alejandro De Aza in the third. Not to be outdone by an infielder, Lorenzo Cain, continuing with his outstanding series, raced toward the wall with two runners on in the third on a ball hit by Nick Hundley, and then as a right fielder in the ninth, chased down a fly ball in foul territory by Cruz.

The first play by Moustakas, the two by Hosmer, and the first by Cain all helped starting pitcher Jeremy Guthrie, who was pitching in a live game for the first time in 12 days. It was the first postseason game for Guthrie, an 11-year veteran who spent 2007–12 with Baltimore. He allowed one run on three hits through five innings.

"Jeremy Guthrie is a pro and a veteran," Yost said. "And he's a guy that you knew that he was going to hold the fort for you. He was going to go out there, and be prepared both physically and mentally, and he was going to try to find a way to get us through five or six innings. He did a great job."

After Guthrie and Frasor got the Royals through six innings, Yost turned the game over to the Royals' Three Musketeers, who pitch as if they've taken the motto "all for one and one for all" to heart this season. Kelvin Herrera and Wade Davis threw perfect seventh and eighth innings, as did Greg Holland, who saved his third game of the ALCS.

"These guys have been tremendous," Holland said of Kansas City's bullpen. "We take pride in expecting to win when the game's tied and we go to the bullpen. We kind of take it as a challenge, as our bullpen versus their bullpen. I know you're facing their hitters, but when it comes to the battle of the bullpens, we take pride in coming out on top."

Yep, "all for one and one for all." And the Royals are one win away from going to the World Series. ■

Wade Davis pitched a perfect eighth inning as the Royals held on to win the rain-delayed third game of the ALCS 2–1. (AP Images)

The Wait Is Over

Dazzling Defense Secures Royals' Spot in World Series

The Royals organization—including its fans—had been waiting 29 years for this moment. They didn't let it pass one more day. Kansas City jumped ahead of Baltimore with two runs in the bottom of the first inning on a chamber of commerce Wednesday afternoon, and went on to beat the Orioles 2-1, clinching the American League title for the first time since 1985 and just the third time in the organization's history.

In the process, the Royals became the first team to start a postseason with eight consecutive wins. Perhaps more shockingly to some—at least to the haters—manager Ned Yost became the first skipper in major league history to win his first eight postseason games.

"This is a wonderful time for America to watch our team," Yost said after the game. "And I think what they've done is they've fallen in love with our team. They love our athleticism. They love our energy. They love the way these guys play hard and enjoy each other. And they love the way that they stand up and get clutch hits and make fantastic plays. And everybody is tipping their cap to each other. They love speed."

All of that was on display from the get-go in Game 4. Sensing a low-scoring game based on the way Game 3 went, the Royals didn't waste any time being aggressive on the base paths. Alcides Escobar led off the Kansas City half of the first with a dribbler over the head of pitcher Miguel Gonzalez. Escobar reached first safely as the ball bounced off the second base bag. Gonzalez then proceeded to hit Nori Aoki on the leg, giving Kansas City runners at first and second with no outs. Lorenzo Cain, who had been outstanding enough both offensively and defensively throughout the series to be selected as the ALCS MVP, put down a sacrifice bunt—on his own and the first of his career—that gave the Royals two runners in scoring position with one out. The next batter, Eric Hosmer, grounded the ball toward first. With Escobar running on contact, first baseman Steve Pearce threw the ball home. The throw seemed to be good enough to get the second out of the inning, but as the ball started to bobble in catcher Caleb Joseph's glove, Escobar knocked it loose and toward the backstop. No one was covering home for the Orioles and the error allowed Aoki to race home for a 2-0 Kansas City lead.

That's all starter Jason Vargas needed. The soft-throwing lefty Vargas, whose only well-pitched game in six weeks was Game 1 of the ALDS against the Angels, kept the Orioles and their potent right-handed hitters off balance.

Alex Gordon leaps toward the left-field wall to catch a ball hit by J.J. Hardy during the fifth inning. Gordon's outfield defense earned the veteran Gold Gloves in 2011, 2012, and 2013. (AP Images)

Baltimore, which led the majors with 211 home runs during the 2014 regular season, had six in the postseason, but only two against Kansas City. Vargas gave up one on a no-doubt shot in the third inning by Ryan Flaherty. Other than that, Vargas gave up only one other hit and three walks in five and one-third innings. A tremendous defensive effort by the Royals certainly didn't hurt, including a play by Alex Gordon in left that will remain embedded in Kansas City baseball history forever.

In the fifth, J.J. Hardy, who was robbed by Cain twice earlier in the series, launched a Vargas pitch toward left that looked like it'd be trouble. Gordon, who sometimes doesn't get enough credit for his athleticism, stepped onto the warning track in a full sprint and leapt back and made the catch as he crashed into the wall and fell to the track. As he went to the ground, Gordon held his glove up to verify he held onto the ball.

"When you range as far as we range in the outfield, Alex Gordon making another spectacular catch today, especially when these games are as tight as they are, you just feel like you're never going to get a break because our defensive guys are absolutely everywhere, and it is a bit deflating," Yost said of the effect Kansas City's defense can have on opponents.

With the Royals leading 2–1 in the sixth and the middle of Baltimore's lineup scheduled to bat, Yost called on the back end of his bullpen—Kelvin Herrera, Wade Davis, and Greg Holland—to close out the game. Each pitcher allowed one base runner, but that was it.

"That's what you dream of as a kid," said Holland, who saved all four games of the ALCS. "Punch your ticket to the World Series, especially before your home crowd. These fans have been waiting a long time. They deserve it."

Or, as Hall of Fame broadcaster Denny Matthews told the radio audience after Hardy ended the game by grounding out to Mike Moustakas: "Kansas City, you have a World Series." ∎

Royals catcher Salvador Perez celebrates after the final out of the Royals' ALCS sweep of the Orioles. (AP Images)

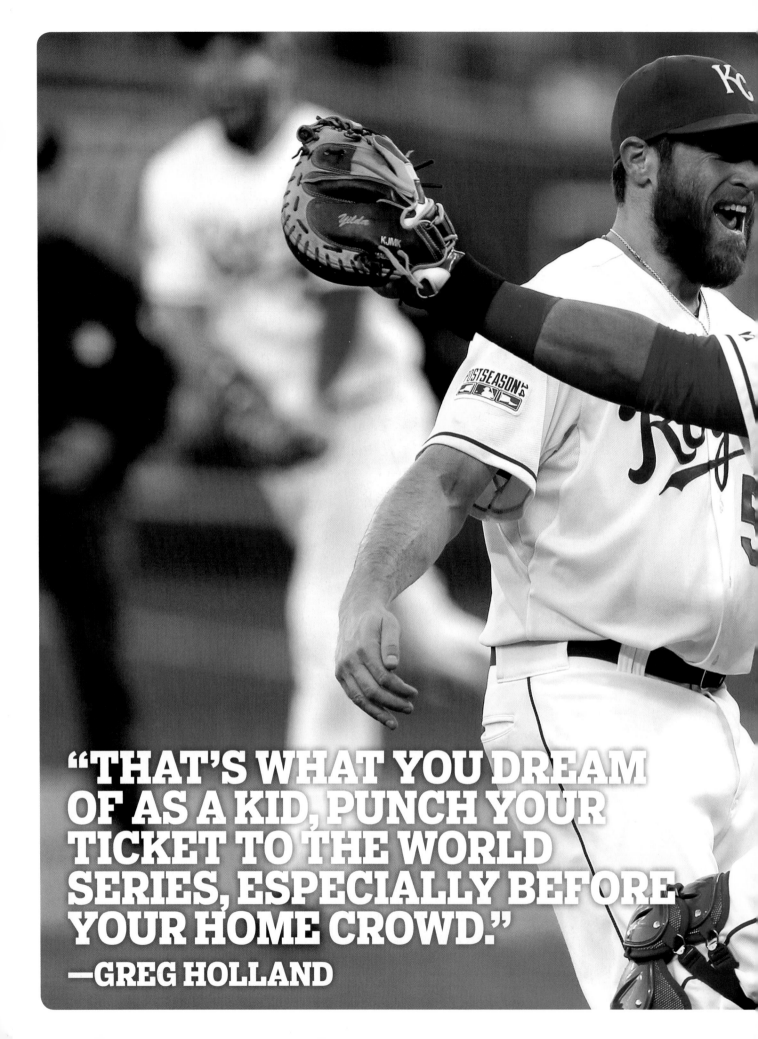

"THAT'S WHAT YOU DREAM OF AS A KID, PUNCH YOUR TICKET TO THE WORLD SERIES, ESPECIALLY BEFORE YOUR HOME CROWD."

—GREG HOLLAND

Closer Greg Holland and catcher Salvador Perez celebrate the Royals' series-clinching 2–1 victory over the Orioles in Game 4. (AP Images)